D0195208

FIVE SMOOTH STONES for PASTORAL WORK

FIVE SMOOTH STONES for PASTORAL WORK

Eugene H. Peterson

John Knox Press
ATLANTA

Unless otherwise indicated Scripture quotations are from the Revised Standard Version of the Holy Bible, copyright, 1946, 1952, and © 1971, 1973 by the Division of Christian Education, National Council of the Churches of Christ in the U.S.A. and used by permission.

Denise Levertov, *The Freeing of the Dust.* Copyright © 1975 by Denise Levertov. Reprinted by permission of New Directions.

Library of Congress Cataloging in Publication Data

Peterson, Eugene H   1932–
  Five smooth stones for pastoral work.

  Includes bibliographical references.
  1. Pastoral theology. 2. Bible. O.T. Five
Scrolls—Use. 3. Bible. O.T. Five Scrolls—
Criticism, interpretation, etc. I. Title.
BV4011.P43   253   79-87751
ISBN 0-8042-1103-5

© copyright John Knox Press 1980
10 9 8 7 6 5 4 3 2 1
Printed in the United States of America
John Knox Press
Atlanta, Georgia 30308

For Russ Reid

ACKNOWLEDGMENTS

"Iron sharpens iron, and one [friend] sharpens another." (Prov. 27:17) Whatever sharpness there is in the pages that follow is a result, first of all, of discussions, challenges, and suggestions among my friends at Christ Our King Presbyterian Church with whom I have worshiped and worked for these seventeen years and among whom I have learned the craft of pastoral work. Other friends who have helped in various ways are Dr. Donald Miller and Dr. Iain Wilson, mentors who gave encouragement and guidance; the Reverend William Hopper, the Reverend John Houdeshel, the Reverend Hugh MacKenzie, and the Reverend Jeffrey Wilson, colleagues in pastoral ministry, whose critical reading of the manuscript improved it immensely; my brother, the Reverend Kenneth Peterson, my sister, Karen Finch, and my wife Janice, who by sharing a commitment to biblically oriented pastoral work have developed and deepened my experience; the insights and affirmations of Russ Reid, close friend for over twenty-five years, were stimulus to both begin and complete the writing. Their sharpening friendships have not always approved but they have always helped.

CONTENTS

INTRODUCTION

Pastoral work takes Dame Religion by the hand and drags her into the everyday world, introducing her to friends, neighbors, and associates. Religion left to herself is shy, retiring, and private; or else she is decorative and proud—a prima donna. But she is not personal and she is not ordinary. The pastor insists on taking her where she must mix with the crowd.

When pastoral work is slighted, religion tends, among some, to become gaudy with ceremonial, among others to get cubbyholed as a private emotion. In either case she still does many things well: her theology can be profound, her meditations mystic, her moral counsels wise, her liturgies splendid. But until she is dragged into the common round she is not alive with Good News nor does she have a chance to put her ideas and beliefs to use, testing them out in actual life-situations.

Pastoral work is that aspect of Christian ministry which specializes in the ordinary. It is the pragmatic application of religion in the present. It has a horror of detachment, neutrality, studious isolation, or theoretic otherworldliness. It is the ministry in mufti.

Pastoral work properly originates, as does all Christian ministry, in the biblical sources. But for at least two generations the perspectives generated by recent behavioral sciences have dominated the literature directed to pastors. The rationale seems to be that since we are in a century of rapid change, that since so much of what we encounter is unprecedented, and that since there have been quantum leaps in knowledge and technology, anything that worked in an earlier age certainly won't work now. We must spend all of our time getting up-to-date. Training must be refashioned. The latest information must be acquired. New techniques must be mastered if we are to be pastors in the age of future shock.

A mood develops in which there is little respect for the past and even less knowledge of it. As the mood envelops pastoral work we are charmed into forgetting the very wisdom that we are called upon to share with others: the majestic reality of God and the immediate significance of each personal and local detail in the story of redemption. We are told that we must be *au courant* in the ways of looking at, studying, and working with persons, and that psychology and sociology will revolutionize our capabilities, putting us in the vanguard of those who will achieve a new human potential. But the work which has to do with the human's relation to God and God's will for the human does not come from knowing more about the times but from knowing humanity—and God. It has to do with continuities, not novelties; with what is essential in the human condition, not with what is accidental. That being the case, we are far more likely to get help from those whose experience has been tested in a variety of climates and cultures, and been demonstrated in the testing to be trustworthy.

When I look for help in developing my pastoral craft and nurturing my pastoral vocation, the one century that has the least to commend it is the twentieth. Has any century been so fascinated with gimmickery, so surfeited with fads, so addicted to nostrums, so unaware of God, so out of touch with the underground spiritual streams which water eternal life? In relation to pastoral work the present-day healing and helping disciplines are like the River Platte as described by Mark Twain, a mile wide and an inch deep. They are designed by a people without roots in an age without purpose for a people without God. The confluence of the sciences of psychology and sociology with the helping professions of the twentieth century is no mystery, for they suit one another admirably. Peter Marin voiced this complaint: "The refusal to consider moral complexities, the denial of history and a larger community, the disappearance of the Other, the exaggerations of the will, the reduction of all experience to a set of platitudes—all of that is to be found in embryonic form in almost all modern therapy."[1] The same complaint can be made in regard to much present-day pastoral work.

It is not uncommon to find pastors who preach and teach biblically. The practice is by no means universal, but it is not rare. The emphases and achievements of the biblical theology movement have observable consequences in pulpits and church schools in most communities in North America. There is quite a different atmosphere, though, in other pastoral work. If in the past fifty years a solid biblical foundation has been rebuilt under pulpit and lectern, it has been consistently eroded in other areas where pastors regularly do their work. If there were once biblical foundations under the pastoral work that is normative between Sundays—work of counsel, guidance, comfort, prayer, administration, community-building—they are not there anymore, or at least they are not there conspicuously.

When I go to my library for instruction and nurture in my preaching and teaching I readily put my hands on volumes by Karl Barth and C. H. Dodd, John Bright and Donald Miller, George Buttrick and David Read, Brevard Childs and Gerhard von Rad. The scholars, theologians, and preachers who lead, support, and encourage me in proclaiming the biblical message and who instruct me in biblically informed understandings of the Christian faith are a magnificent company. If at any point I have failed to preach and teach biblically I have no one to blame but myself. No generation in the church's history has been so blessed with as devout and biblical a scholarship. But when I get up on Monday to face a week of parish routine I am handed books by Sigmund Freud and Abraham Maslow, Marshall McLuhan and Talcott Parsons, John Kenneth Galbraith and Lewis Mumford. It is a literature of humanism and technology. The pulpit is grounded in the prophetic and kerygmatic traditions but the church office is organized around IBM machines. The act of teaching is honed on biblical insights derived from historical, grammatical, form, and redaction criticism while the hospital visit is shaped under the supervision of psychiatrists and physicians. The sociologists, psychologists, management consultants, and community organizers of the twentieth century are brilliant. Their insights are dazzling and their instruction useful. I have profited a great deal under their tutelage, but am I ill at ease still. I can demonstrate acceptable competence in the skills I have been taught, but am I a *pastor?* I function adequately in a variety of dovetailed roles, but is there a biblical foundation providing solid, authoritative underpinning for what I am doing so that my daily work is congruent with the ancient ministries of prophet, priest, and wise man to which I am heir? My instructors frequently lift a text from the Bible to assure me that they are on my side, but the plain fact is that I never seem to meet pastoral companions, living or dead, in the culture that they nurture. Saving history, covenantal theology, incarnational thinking are on the periphery of their concerns and unacknowledged in their expertise. They teach me to be facile in playing roles and to be nimble in changing them. The pastoral work that results is not lacking in skills or usefulness—but I have little sense that it is indigenous to the world of faith, no feeling of having my practice develop from within the biblical world. I pick and choose my way through the books and articles, the lectures and seminars, cutting and pasting, plundering and salvaging anything that I think I can use. There is, of course, a great deal to be used.

Still, I am not satisfied. Having accepted the counsel of my contemporaries and having done what they have told me to do, I find that I want more. I want more than intelligent advice and competent training. I want a biblical base for the whole of pastoral ministry, and not just its preaching and teaching.

1

It is the unique property of pastoral work to combine two aspects of ministry: one, to represent the eternal word and will of God; and, two, to do it among the idiosyncrasies of the local and the personal (the actual *place* where the pastor lives; the named *people* with whom he or she lives). If either aspect is slighted, good pastoral work fails to take place. At its best such pastoral work narrates and models the biblically described exchanges of grace between God who is "the same yesterday, today, and forever" and the person who inherits old Adam's sin and experiences new Adam's salvation. In these exchanges the gift of God is consistent and the need of the person constant. Between the fixed poles of God's gift and the person's need there are variables. They occur in such a way that they cannot be charted on a graph showing a line through history of either ascent or decline. There are, simply, repeated instances, "cases," of interaction between the will of God and the will of persons. There are no lines of progress in pastoral work along which later generations reach new levels, outdistancing and outmoding their predecessors. What we find instead is depth: rich layers of accumulated evidence, some of it sifted out as wisdom.[2] Many have made it their task to labor at the pastoral nexus in the divine economy—pastoral work operates out of a long tradition in Israel and church. It is essential to stay in touch, almost literally, with the biblical material and pastoral traditions where specific God-person exchanges take place. The Greek story of Antaeus is a myth of warning. Antaeus, one of the giant offspring of Mother Earth, always slept on the bare ground in order to conserve and increase his already colossal strength. When ever he touched the earth, his strength revived. Hercules, in a wrestling match with the giant, noticed that every time he got the best of him and threw him to the ground, the giant's muscles swelled and a healthy flush suffused his limbs as Mother Earth revived him. So Hercules threw him down no more but held him high in the air, cracking his ribs one by one until he died. If pastoral work is removed from its ground it loses, like Antaeus, the strength to grapple with the complexities inherent in the work. Separation, by ignorance or forgetfulness, from the biblical pastoral traditions is responsible for two parodies of pastoral work: one, the naive attempt to help people on our own, as best we can, out of the natural compassion and concern we have for them; and two, the insensitive harangues from the pulpit, where, safe from the unmanageable am biguities of bedroom and kitchen, shopping mall and workshop, corporate board room and legislative caucus, we confidently declaim the pure word of God to our confused flock. The Bible has the power to prevent either parody, either the naive humanist absorption *into* the world, or the pseudo-spiritual aloofness *from* the world. The Bible's paradigmatic interchanges of divine and human reality inform and renew pastoral capabilities so that the work can be practiced among the commonplaces of sin with no loss of the extraordinariness of grace. But if that is to be done the idea of quick achievement and instant exploitation must be abandoned in order to develop, painstakingly, lives in Christ that are coherent and many-dimensioned.

Donald G. Miller writes:

The Bible is the prime requisite for our pastoral ministry. There is nothing more difficult to do than to deal intimately with people in personal relations. It is much easier to preach. Somebody once asked Gregory of Nazianzus a question. He replied, "I would rather answer that one in the pulpit!" It is easier to deal with men's needs in the mass in the sacred enclosure of the pulpit than to face them alone in the intimate relationship of a pastoral visit.[3]

The present age, though, gives pastors little encouragement to keep in touch with this biblical heritage. America does not honor the quiet work that develops spiritual root systems and community stability. To avoid being swept along by the winds of change and conducting a ministry which is mostly improvisation, one must stubbornly dig one's heels into the ground. For it takes no skill to be "current"— to be in tune with what is going on in the world. Scattered conversations with neurotic, compulsive, depressed, and ambitious men and women through the day, supplemented with twenty minutes of newspaper reading in the morning and half an hour of television viewing in the evening keeps me in touch with what is "modern." The glib criticism that pastors in the twentieth century are out of touch with the times is, to me, not credible. The times are the very things we are in touch with.

I am in no way contemptuous of modern culture. I enjoy it and participate in it. It is the environment in which I have learned the love of Christ and the territory in which I share the work of Christ. At the same time, though, I am quite certain that it is a mistake to look for nutrients for my pastoral vocation from the stuff of the American twentieth century. Saul Bellow's Charlie Citrine is an accurate observer: "Maybe America didn't need art and inner miracles. It had so many outer ones. The USA was a big operation, very big. The more *it,* the less *we.* "[4] Which means that our culture is thinnest in the very areas in which I need the most help. I need encouragement to attend to God with steadfast faithfulness and the patience to immerse myself in the local and the personal. But our society marshals enormous resources and ingenuity to *make things happen.* Immense stores of knowledge can be computerized and used in scientific enterprises that boggle the mind. But the very persons who are doing these things are not in any sense "wise," that is, skilled in living. The scientists who put men on the moon cannot get along with their own wives and children. The politicians who impressively balance power struggles on an international scale are alienated from those who live closely with them. The artists who give us a "vision of reality" are full of rascality themselves.

> The twentieth century may have its epiphanies but it is not a favorable time for the greater visions and wider circumspections. Its intellectuals especially are out of their depth in dealing with those dimensions of experience for which earlier epochs have found a language.[5]

They are also out of touch with the particulars of creation and locales of redemption, having been swept away on the generalizations of mass movements and the impersonalizations of institutionalized work. This does not discredit their science, or politics, or art, or scholarship. It does, though, disqualify them as instructors in wisdom, that is, giving sound counsel in living whole and worthy lives in the context of God's creation and in response to Christ's redemption, which is the task assigned to pastoral work.

One might have supposed that a person who had learned to read Hebrew and Greek and been immersed in the sacred scriptures with the thoroughness that reading them in their original tongues requires, might be innoculated against fads. And one might suppose that one who had pondered the centuries-long story of a people's salvation, meditated the passion of Christ, and been instructed in the theology of Paul, would not be easily lured from such moorings to make mythological guesses with clues provided by the story of Oedipus, or attempt to understand the children of God on models recently derived from the mentally ill, or be captivated by the murky prose of pretenders to the scientific method, but it has happened. Pastors are more likely to be conversant with the gestalt therapy of Frederick Perls than with the confessional prayers of Jeremiah of Anathoth. They are more adept at quoting Ralph Nader of Washington on consumer rip-offs than Isaiah of Jerusalem on peace. They are more enthusiastic over the reformism of Ivan Illich than over the reformer John Calvin. They are far more appreciative of and knowledgeable in the gnostic archetypes of Carl Jung than in the courageous arguments of Martin Luther. The Bible we use on Sundays is quickly replaced on Monday by the current organizational manual or counseling handbook or editorial insight. But pastoral work gathers expertise not by acquiring new knowledge but by assimilating old wisdom, not by reading the latest books but by digesting the oldest ones. "Knowledge is not intelligence."[6] Since the work deals with what is local and essential in humankind—our relationships with God in a daily existence defined *sub specie aeternitatis*—the accumulated experience of those who have paid attention to and worked with these relationships most diligently holds the best promise for nurture. And since our age, cyclonic with change, does not encourage such an approach, deliberate effort must be directed to the old continuities in pastoral work. Otherwise we float on fads; or we develop pastoral strategies in response to the fake little cycles of death and rebirth which are monitored by the seasonal rise and fall of the hemline. Too much pastoral work in our time is a consequence of that kind of procedure—a gerry-built structure, hastily and desperately put together out of whatever is at hand from the graduate schools, the bestseller lists, and the latest opinion poll listings of what people want. "We deplore most of all," write Clebsch and Jaekle as they attempt to give historical depth to pastoral work, "the growing sense of discontinuity."[7] Meanwhile scripture is at hand for those who will use it, foundation stones upon which a better pastoral work can be constructed.

2

In approaching scripture thus it is important to maintain a distinction between biblical foundation and pastoral superstructure. For there is not much pastoral work in scripture that can be taken over, as is, into a pastor's routines. Pastoral work is complex, a vast mixture of things in which the revelation of God in Christ and creation is put to work in what William Golding has called the " 'ordinary universe.' "[8] Since each culture, each generation, and each congregation has aspects of individuality, each generation of pastors, and to a certain extent each pastor, has to build his or her own superstructure of pastoral work. But we don't, and we must not, lay out our own foundations.

Pastors coming to scripture in search of foundation stones for their work are somewhat like those ancient peoples, whose histories are reconstructed for us by archeologists, who returned to a village after it had been destroyed. The sites for villages and cities were usually chosen for agricultural or strategic reasons. The place had access to water, or was easily defended against marauders, or, preferably, both. The homes and sanctuaries and city walls that were constructed on such sites were, with fair regularity, destroyed. Sometimes the destruction was the result of natural disaster—fire or earthquake. Sometimes by military invasion. The city would be left in rubble. But not for long. Because it was a good place for living the people would come back and rebuild. The new city would look different from the old. Sometimes the returning people would have learned a new design for building from the Philistines, or Cypriotes, or Egyptians and would build in a different style. Sometimes they would have learned something about improving fortifications and would build the new wall thicker and stronger. In the rebuilding they would use the materials that were already there—the old foundation stones—and they would build on the same site. As archeologists probe these layers of habitation they find the same foundation patterns and the same foundation stones used over and over and over again by successive generations of inhabitants.

Persons who are called to do pastoral work at this time in history are very much, it seems to me, in the position of those ancient peoples who, after a time of destruction, straggle back to the ruins and wonder how they are going to put it back together again. Pastoral traditions and pastoral craft have been smashed beyond recognition. We are in the country of Psalm 74:

> the enemy has destroyed everything in the sanctuary!
> . . . .
> At the upper entrance they hacked
>   the wooden trellis with axes.
> And then all its carved wood
>   they broke down with hatchets and hammers.
> They set thy sanctuary on fire;
>   to the ground they desecrated the dwelling place of thy name.
> they burned all the meeting places of God in the land.
> We do not see our signs. (Ps. 74: 3–9)

The well-wrought craftsmanship of pastoral visitation in Richard Baxter, for instance, where is that? The practiced skill in spiritual letter writing that is in Samuel Rutherford, where is that? The "passion of patience," surely one of the requisite skills for pastoral work, that is in Newman in the oratory at Birmingham, where is that? Instead of subtly nuanced abilities in pastoral visitation we get training in mass visitation movements, misnamed evangelism, that promise to fill the pews on Sundays. Instead of letters of spiritual counsel we get slogans designed for the mass media. Instead of models for patience we get pep talks and cheerleader yells to work up church spirit. And if our lumpish congregations refuse to wave their pompoms on signal, we stalk off to another congregation, and another, until we find some people dumb enough to put up with such inanities

> We do not see our signs;
>   there is no longer any prophet,
>   and there is none among us who knows how long.
> How long, O God, is the foe to scoff?
> Is the enemy to revile thy name for ever? (Ps. 74:9-10)

But we are not the first people to stand over the rubble and wonder which stone to put where in the rebuilding work. The "tell" of pastoral work is a considerable mound on the plain of ministry. And the strata of occupation are clear: there is an Augustinian layer, a Benedictine layer, a Franciscan layer, a Lutheran layer, a Calvinist layer, a Wesleyan layer, a Kierkegaardian layer—all using biblical stones. The one thing we must not do is wander off and try to find a new building site. The rebuilding must be done on the biblical site, using the biblical foundation stones.

There are any number of biblical documents at hand for doing this work. Deuteronomy, for instance, shows the marks of being used in this way more than once. Deuteronomy is a document which takes the old patriarchal and exodus traditions, reworks them in a new setting and puts them to pastoral use in the age of Josiah. Matthew is an instance of the way in which the early kerygmatic and didactic materials of the apostolic age are shaped to pastoral use by the messianic community, the church. And there are others.

Among these other, more modest materials, are the Megilloth, the five scrolls in the Hebrew Bible that we recognize under the names of Song of Songs, Ruth, Lamentations, Ecclesiastes, and Esther. They are, perhaps, the least pretentious of all the books in the Bible. None has any particular claim to greatness. They are not in the same class as the Law or the Prophets. Some of them barely achieved canonical status at all. All the same, they *are* in the Bible. Lloyd Bailey reminds us that

> ... *every* story in the Bible presupposes a believing community whose identity was (in some measure) affirmed and sustained by it. Thus the story was repeated, handed down, treasured (i e , canonized) by the communal wisdom of the generations: It has been "tried" by our history and found worthy.[9]

The appropriateness of the Megilloth as documents for pastoral work is suggested by their use in Judaism where we find that they are assigned readings at five of Israel's annual acts of worship. At these festivals God's people gathered from all the villages of Palestine and from across the roads of the diaspora to remember who they were, to find the motivation and direction for continuing their lives of praise and obedience and faith, to orient their lives in the words and acts of God. Which is to say, they came to *worship.* The Megilloth did not define these occasions; they did not even interpret them. But during the festival it became customary for someone to get up and read the assigned scroll. Each reading had the effect of nourishing one aspect of the life of the people who were committed to live in covenant with their God. The scrolls were the applied wisdom of the pastoral office to a people who had come together to pay attention to their life together with God. Song of Songs was read at Passover, Ruth at Pentecost, Lamentations on the Ninth of Ab, Ecclesiastes at Tabernacles, and Esther at Purim.

The assignment of these five scrolls to the five annual acts of worship (four festivals and a fast) has seemed to me to be a singular stroke of pastoral imagination. No one knows who did it, or even when it was done. The first documentary evidence of the practice comes from the eighth and ninth centuries A.D., although some scholars conjecture that the practice began as early as the period of the Second Temple. By setting the scrolls, in turn, in the specific kerygmatic settings of worship, remarkable and somewhat unexpected insights for pastoral work were released. And what was done once can be done again.

In reusing the Megilloth for present day pastoral work we are using scripture in the same way that Israel did, over and over again —taking seriously what is handed down as the word and act of God, treating it with respect, meditating its meaning, and then using it in the contemporary situation, believing and living it in the present. We are not trying to stuff modern pastoral life into an ancient mold in order to "shape it up" biblically; we are simply trying to stay in touch with the vitalities of good pastoral work which are evident in the biblical materials and then put them to use in our own present.

The recycling of scripture is itself a biblical process. Israel did it all the time. She never simply repeated her history, cyclically. Each generation carried some things over, ignored some aspects, and introduced, occasionally, innovations. There is both dependence upon tradition and freedom within it. Every page of scripture shows that it happened and in some instances how it happened. For instance, the "god of the fathers" was taken and reshaped by Yahwism. The traditions of Zion and David were preached and developed in fresh ways by Isaiah. The experience of Exodus and the leadership of Moses were put to new and original uses by Deuteronomy. The elements of the old were creatively used in realizing the divine promise and the people's vocation in the present. Ezekiel (in chapter 20) gives a completely original interpretation of the venerable traditions of the Exodus and the events of the wilderness period, so that they are workable in the exile realities of the sixth century. Nearly every page of both Old and New Testaments shows the results of this creative handling of old traditions, every generation making a fresh, interpretive start, and yet in such a way that nothing is lost. The making of scripture and the formation of the canon are in some ways a demonstration of what C. S. Lewis announced on the first page of his *Allegory of Love:* "Humanity does not pass through phases as a train passes through stations: being alive, it has the privilege of always moving yet never leaving anything behind. Whatever we have been, in some sort we are still."[10]

Gerhard von Rad has shown in detail how "this process of adapting older traditions to suit the new situation was the most legitimate way by which Israel was able to preserve the continuity of her history with God and prevent it from disintegrating into a series of unrelated acts."[11]

There is a sense, then, in which all pastoral work is redactional, a reworking of scriptural preaching and teaching for the sake of the present community, combining kerygmatic faithfulness with pastoral sensitivity.

Each of the Megilloth, set by Judaism in an act of worship, deals with an aspect of pastoral work: learning how to love and pray in the context of salvation (Song of Songs); developing an identity as a person of faith in the context of God's covenant (Ruth); dealing with suffering in the context of redemptive judgment (Lamentations); unmasking religious illusion and pious fraud in the context of providential blessing (Ecclesiastes); and becoming a celebrative community of faith in the environment of the world's hostility (Esther). Not everything a pastor does fits into the five areas, but a remarkable amount of it does, giving promise that the Megilloth may be highly serviceable for pastoral use. The Megilloth are not, it must be said, cornerstones for such construction—that would be too much to claim for them. But neither are they inconsequential pebbles. They are both substantial and useful as foundation stones under pastoral work.

3

Worship is the setting in which the Megilloth are discovered to be useful for pastoral work. Read and studied in their historical settings the Megilloth develop one set of interpretations. Listened to in the midst of an act of worship (Passover, Pentecost, Ninth of Ab, Tabernacles, Purim) they develop meanings which are quite different. A precious stone embedded in a stratum of rock has one appearance. After it is mined, cut, polished, and set in a ring which is then worn on a hand, it is quite different in both function and appearance, although not different in substance. By setting the Megilloth in prescribed acts of worship, Judaism brought out effects which were not apparent in the historical settings, giving pastoral direction and insight and demonstrating pastoral function. Nothing new is added, but what is there is perceived in a *pastoral* way.

By using the Megilloth in the context of community worship Judaism demonstrated what continues to be true in both Israel and church: pastoral work has its origin in the act of worship. Community ("common") worship is the biblical setting for pastoral work. Nor is it possible to do pastoral work apart from common worship. Pastoral work has no identity in and of itself. It is a derivative work and worship is that from which it is derived.

In worship the community of God's people assemble to hear God's word spoken in scripture, sermon, and sacrament. The faith which is created by that proclaimed word develops responses of praise, obedience, and commitment. At no time has there ever been a biblical faith, or any kind of continuing life in relation to God, apart from such common worship. By persisting in the frequent, corporate worship in which God's word is central, God's people are prevented from making up a religion out of their own private ideas of God. They are also prevented from making a private, individualized salvation out of what they experience, separating themselves from brothers and sisters with whom God has made it clear his saving love is to be shared, both in receiving and giving.

All pastoral work originates in this act of worship. Each Lord's Day the pastor speaks the invitational command, "Let us worship God." But the work does not terminate an hour later with the pronouncing of the benediction, for pastoral work also accompanies the people as they live out what they have heard and sung and said and believed in worship. Pastoral work takes place between Sundays, between the first and the eighth day, between the boundaries of creation and resurrection, between Genesis 1 and Revelation 21. Sunday worship establishes the life of the community of faith in and on the word of God; weekday pastoral work unfolds the implications in the ordinary lives of people as they work, love, suffer, grieve, play, learn, and grow in times of crisis and times of routine. Worship calls a congregation to attention before God's words, coordinates responses of praise and obedience, and then sends the people out into the community to live out the meaning of that praise and obedience. But they are not only sent, they are accompanied, and pastoral

[margin note: solid definition of worship]

work is the ministry of that accompaniment. Pastoral work begins at
the Pulpit, the Font, the Table; it continues in the hospital room, the
family room, the counseling room, the committee room. The pastor
who leads people in worship is companion to those same people
between acts of worship.

Any pastoral act that is severed from the common worship slowly
but certainly loses its biblical character.[12] It becomes an isolated act
of healing, of comforting, of guiding, of ordering—a cut-flower
ministry, lovely but limp. It is, of course, still useful insofar as it is
done well, but separated from its biblical origins it fails to participate
in the unfolding of the kerygmatic realities which builds the wholeness that God intends for his creation.

The five Megilloth, set in five acts of Israelite worship, demonstrate ways in which the kerygmatic traditions that are announced
and embraced in worship are continued and nurtured in the daily
round. These scrolls pick up areas in which sin typically distorts,
obscures, or avoids the gospel realities proclaimed in the act of
worship and provides the correctives, disciplines, and insights that
keep them personal and real. Used in such settings they become
pastoral documents.

4

High on the agenda for the rebuilding of a biblical pastoral work
is the acquisition of facility in the idiom of the local, the specific, and
the personal. T. S. Eliot, writing in regard to other matters, once
said:

> "A local speech on a local issue is likely to be more intelligible than
> one addressed to a whole nation, and we observe that the greatest
> muster of ambiguities and obscure generalities is usually to be found
> in speeches which are addressed to the whole world."[13]

Each of the Megilloth is "a local speech on a local issue," and for
that reason is a working model for the pastoral work which is called
to encourage the clarities of specific obedience and nurture the
particularities of weekday faith.

The pastor, walking through the high country of the great gospel
proclamations and assemblies, comes on the Megilloth as a hiker

comes on trail snacks and campfires—localized instances of refreshment and recovery in an environment of grandeur. However magnificent the alpine vistas one can't always be exclaiming over them. There is fatigue to deal with and basic needs to be met. It is the pastor's task to work along such trails using a style of speech and a mode of action that is local, specific, and personal so that each person met is addressed as an object of the love of God which is not merely universal but particular in its universality, for, as Barth reminds us, the Holy Spirit of ministry "is not an anonymous magnitude and force"[14] but wholly specific and always personal. The Megilloth are five instances of what it means to attend to these details of pastoral work in the modest, limited, transitory, and ordinary places where pastors are called to work between Sundays.

The
PASTORAL WORK
of
PRAYER-DIRECTING:
SONG of SONGS

In certain states of romantic love the Holy Spirit has deigned to reveal, as it were, the Christ-hood of two individuals each to other. He is himself the *conciliator* and it is there that the "conciliation"—and the Reconciliation —begins. But this is possible only because of the Incarnation, because "matter is capable of salvation," because the *anthropos* is united with the *theos,* and because the natural and the supernatural are one Christ.
—Charles Williams[1]

She came to see me at the recommendation of a friend. She had been troubled for years, seeing psychiatrists *seriatim* and not getting any better. The consultation had been arranged on the telephone so that when she walked into my study it was a first meeting. Her opening statement was, "Well, I guess you want to know all about my sex life—that's what they always want to know." I answered, "If that is what you want to talk about I'll listen. What I would really be interested in finding out about, though, is your prayer life."

She didn't think I was serious, but I was. I was interested in the details of her prayer life for the same reason that her psychiatrists had been interested in the details of her sex life—to find out how she handled intimate relationships. I had to settle for the details of her sex life at that time. Sex was the only language she knew for describing relationships of intimacy. At a later time, when she came to understand herself in relation to a personal God, she also learned to use the language of prayer.

I like to tell the story because it juxtaposes two things that crisscross constantly in pastoral work: sexuality and prayer. And it juxtaposes them in such a way as to show that they are both aspects of a single, created thing: a capacity for intimacy.

Wow!

Much of pastoral work has to do with nurturing intimacy, that is, developing relationships in which love is successfully expressed and received—shared. The relationships are multiform: between woman and man, husband and wife, parent and child, sisters and brothers, neighbors and acquaintances, employers and employees, friends and enemies, rich and poor, sinners and saints. And, in addition to but also involved in each of these combinations, the person and God. All horizontal relationships between other persons, when they achieve any degree of intimacy at all, are aspects of sexuality. All vertical relationships with persons of the Godhead, when there is any degree of intimacy at all, involve prayer. And since there are never instances of merely horizontal relationships and never any solely vertical relationships—we are created in both directions; there are no one-dimensional beings—both sexuality and prayer (or *either* sexuality *or* prayer) can be used to explore and develop personal relationships of intimacy. Either, used thus, involves the other. When we develop and express our love to another person we are using the same words and actions and emotions that also are used to develop and express our love for God; and vice versa.

And so it happens that the person who comes to the pastor because of a difficulty in human relationships is led to a comprehension and understanding of God's place in our existence, is encouraged in faith and taught to pray. The person who comes to the pastor full of anxiety about a spiritual condition is led to see the connection between God's will and the other persons who live in the same house or neighborhood or place of work, and learns how to express the connection in acts of forgiveness, of compassion, of affection, of witness, of service.

What Pastors are about

Pastors are assigned the task of helping persons develop their everyday relationships in such a way that they discover God's will and love at the center of every encounter. We are also given the correlative task of training persons in mature discipleship so that what is believed in the heart has demonstrable consequences in daily life. In some ways it matters little where you start: with the physical relationships as an analogy of the spiritual or with the spiritual as a model for the personal. Regardless of where you start, it is only a step or two to get from one to the other. Because of the common origin of our creation and redemption, an examination of our sex life leads to an examination of our prayer life and vice versa.[2]

When pastors leave the pulpits on Sunday, we don't, overnight, turn into humanists on Monday, our Sunday prayers and preaching serving as only a vague and wispy background for the real work of helping people. Nor do we, during the week, collar all the people we meet and lead them to the altar to "get them right with God." There are some, of course, who do: who apart from their pulpits, having left all theological ballast behind, plunge with great good will into the sea of human need; or who apart from their pulpits are incapacitated for any work at all except that of repeating snatches of their Sunday sermon to whomever they might meet. Biblical pastoral work, though, is not permitted to disfigure ministry with such barbarities.

We live in a whole world of creation and redemption in which all the relationships which stretch along a continuum of sexual identity and spiritual capacity are involved in our daily growth and discipleship. Pastoral work refuses to specialize in earthly or heavenly, human or divine. The pastor is given a catholic cosmos to work in, not a sectarian back-forty.

Salvation

not only with God but also with man, + with woman

The personal relationships for which we were created and in which we are confused because of our sin, are re-created (redeemed) by salvation. Salvation is the act of God in which we are rescued from the consequences of our sin (bondage, fragmentation) and put in a position to live in free, open, loving relationships with God and our neighbors. The double command "love God . . . love your neighbor . . ." assumes salvation as a background. *Without* God's act of salvation we are "dead in trespasses and sin." *With* God's act of salvation we are able to be addressed by a whole series of commands by which we are ordered into live, whole, healthy relationships with God and other persons.

The most pondered act of salvation in Israel was the Exodus. It was *the* great act in which she experienced God as Savior and herself as saved. The event was the kerygmatic center to all of Hebrew life —a glad proclamation of the dynamic action by which it was now possible to live with meaning and in praise before a holy and living God. This kerygma was preserved in the Feast of Passover. The annual repetition of the feast kept the memory fresh. In ritual meal, storytelling and psalms-singing, the deliverance from Egyptian slavery and inauguration into new life as a free people of God was relived, understood, and sung within the domestic environs of the family. The people were *saved*—they were defined, shaped, and centered not by military, political, or environmental forces but by the act of God. Salvation was God acting decisively in history so that each person, both individually and corporately, was free to live in faith. Salvation—God doing for us what we cannot do for ourselves, overcoming the powers of bondage, leading through the forces of evil, establishing the people in fact as God's beloved—was announced in the Feast of Passover as present and personal.

The salvation story, as it takes form in the Exodus narrative, is awesome and majestic. No story is more memorable in the life of God's people and is only surpassed among Christians by Easter, a final and completed Exodus. The devout and grateful mind of Israel returned over and over again to the event, remembering, understanding, praising, and responding. The story mixes elements of miracle and the mundane in combinations that set the imagination reeling: the majesty of God and the misery of the people, the stuttering tongue of Moses, the hard heart of Pharaoh, the victory over what everyone supposed were invincible political powers (the Egyptians) and unassailable physical obstacles (the Sea of Reeds). But, however awesome, it was unmistakably historical: it occurred in datable time and locatable space and therefore had consequences in present time and space. No one ever supposed it was a timeless myth that could be used (or not used) to "understand" human existence;

Exodus
historical event

it was a historical event that demonstrated beyond argument that God saved his people.

By preaching this act of salvation at the annual Feast of Passover, the people repeatedly came to terms with the hard-edged historical reality that they owed their present existence to an act of God which rescued them from that to which they were doomed, that set them in a new way of life against all worldly odds, and that made them whole for a life of faith. The word "salvation" in the course of its biblical usage developed both the sense of "rescue from destruction" and "restoration to health."[3]

Salvation means to be whole again, to be delivered in the midst of peril. Far back toward the Hebrew root of the word, it may even suggest that no matter how closely the evil hedges you about, God will yet clear for you all the space you need to move around it: "I called upon the LORD in distress: the LORD answered me, *and set me in a large place.*" (Ps. 118:5 K.J.V.) Passover was the concentrated, annual attention that Israel gave to God's definitive act of saving love.

But the repetition of the celebration carried with it a danger, the danger that salvation itself should be ritualized and institutionalized. The Passover ritual which was designed to represent the great impossibilities and indescribable realities of grace, was, after all, very visible. It was acted out by the wise and the foolish, the bright and the dull, the pious and the impious, year after year whether these persons felt like it or not. That which was charged with creative power in the beginning, through the years and with each repetition of the ritual, was in danger of becoming a shell, a husk of reality. If that continued, there would come a time when the entire nation would experience only the ritual and not the reality, knowing only the institution and not the salvation.

In order to protect against this danger someone with pastoral genius assigned the Song of Songs for reading at Passover. The central act of Passover celebration is the eating of a ritual meal. The meal concludes with the reading of the Song of Songs.[4] The reading, of course, was not originally a part of the feast; the feast was kept long before the Song was written. But at some point the Song was assigned as a concluding reading to the *seder,* the Passover meal.

That assignment was clearly a pastoral act. The reading of the Song in the context of Passover is a demonstration that the glorious once-for-all historical event of salvation in which God's people are established in the way of God's love is workable in the everyday domestic settings of intimacy between persons. It bridges the transition from Exodus event to daily activities so that there is no loss of wonder, intensity, or joy. The Song is the most inward, the most intimate, the most personal of all the biblical books (excepting, perhaps, The Psalms). It complements the historical re-enactment with a personal reparticipation. It draws attention from the historical setting to the inward relationships. No lyrics, ancient or modern, communicate the intimacies and the exuberances of being whole and good in relation to another—that is of being saved—more convincingly than the Song.

Lloyd R. Bailey has called attention to the fact "That sacred texts are not randomly to be read, but that each has its proper occasion and combination with other texts . . . an idea well attested in the ancient world including Israel and her neighbors."[5] Theodore H. Gaster in *Thespis*[6] cites the example of the recitation of the creation story *(Enuma Elish)* that must take place during the late afternoon of the fourth day of the New Year celebration at Babylon.[7] The combination of Song of Songs and Passover is thoroughly appropriate, and especially noteworthy for pastors who are committed to nurturing devotional intimacies and relational wholeness—the personal, immediate, experiential aspects of the gospel in the context of salvation.

Pastoral work, in large part, deals with the difficulty everyone has in staying alert to the magnificence of salvation. When we first encounter God's saving love, it may well overwhelm us. But over a period of years it becomes a familiar part of the landscape, one religious item among many others. The vocabulary of salvation becomes hackneyed, reduced to the level of valentine-card verse. The mannerisms of the saved become predictable. Whenever we are associated with greatness over a long period of time, there is a tendency in us to become stale. What we first experienced (in our faith, in our marriage, in our children, in our career, in the landscape) as earthshaking and soul-changing vision and adventure, we now take for granted. We lose, in the language of the Apocalypse, our "first love." We preserve its importance by assigning the event a date on the calendar or by describing it under a doctrinal head. Orthodoxy is preserved even while intimacy is lost. The pastor, working in the midst of the symbols and artifacts of transcendence, is faced, both in himself or herself and among the faithful, with this dangerous drift towards the shoals of nonchalance. Praying, the most personal aspect of life, becomes riddled with cliches, a sure indication that it has ceased being personal. Devotional life diminishes while a step-up in public and external activities (church work, defending the faith, witnessing and preaching, moral formalisms) covers up the loss. So-called "ordinary Christians" assume that the great spiritual experiences are for the great Christians; that the tremendous gospel events are for crisis times; that Easter comes only once a year. It is not difficult to fill a church sanctuary on Easter; it is not difficult to demonstrate the overwhelming reality of the resurrection. But the pastor's task is to gather people together *every* Sunday, center *each* week in a response to the risen Lord, and nurture a participation in the resurrection life in Christ that works as well on any Wednesday afternoon at 5 o'clock as on Easter at sunrise.

(handwritten margin note: we hardly do that with our spouses)

(handwritten margin note: The Pastor's task)

This is one of the boundaries at which pastoral life is lived out: the boundary between religious ritual and personal love, between the institution and the personal. The pastor deals with people in the context of the historical and institutional, but always in order to bring about personal, intimate participation in the saving love which is ritualized in the forms of worship and the disciplines of the institution. That which begins in the prayer and praise and preaching of worship continues in pastoral work: the rescue operation that is announced in the gospel of salvation becomes a health operation in the way of pastorally guided discipleship.

The Song of Songs functions as a pastoral document by taking up the theme of saving love, the kind of love that rescues from nonbeing and creates being-in-relationship, and exploring, in exuberant detail, its daily intimacies. Life-changing love, massive and overpowering in the history of the Exodus, is celebrated in the domesticities of personal relationship in language everyone can understand and in an experience that is no farther away than the bedroom. The love lyrics of the Song are a guard against every tendency to turn living faith into a lifeless "religion." They make sure that as we proclaim the truth *of* God, we do not exclude faith *in* God. The Song provides correctives to our tendencies to reduce faith to a tradition, or to make an academic dogma of it. It insists that however impressive the acts of God and however exalted the truths of God, they are not too great or too high to be experienced by ordinary people in the minutiae of the everyday.

The preacher in the pulpit proclaims the acts of salvation in the event of Exodus: a whole people is redeemed out of slavery; a treacherous sea passage is negotiated miraculously; God saves his people—by grace! The pastor in the parish has the responsibility of insisting that the Exodus event continues to be a design for salvation to the person who does piecework in a factory, to the youth who pumps gasoline, to the woman in daily negotiation with the demands of diapers and career, to the man trying to achieve poise between ambition in his profession and sensitivity to his wife and children at home. Pastoral work is a commitment to the everyday: it is an act of faith that the great truths of salvation are workable in the "ordinary universe."

Adam

Karl Barth provides the exegetical foundation for using The Song of Songs in such pastoral work. In his exegesis of Genesis 2 he examines the sexual nature of humanity, "created male and female," and demonstrates that the human being is created in such a way that covenantal relationships can be engaged and developed.[8] Much of what follows from Genesis 2 in the Bible tells of the disruption of this covenantal base. Sexual metaphors are used in the Bible most frequently to describe humanity's unwillingness and inability to sustain a faithful love relationship with the faithful God of love. Adultery and harlotry are the usual metaphors for describing humankind's role in the covenant. In other words, the well-known disturbance and corruption in the relationships of the sexes is used to describe the sin-crossed relations of people with God. The work of salvation takes place in the ruins of broken commitments and the rubble of deteriorated loyalties. The prophets spoke the indictments repeatedly. Three representative prophets from the eighth, seventh, and sixth centuries, respectively, use similar language.

Hosea, in the eighth century:

> They shall eat, but not be satisfied;
>   they shall play the harlot, but not multiply;
> because they have forsaken the LORD
>   to cherish harlotry. (Hosea 4:10)
> For the spirit of harlotry is within them
>   and they know not the LORD. (Hosea 5:4)
> They are all adulterers. (Hosea 7:4)

Jeremiah in the seventh century:

> "Lift up you eyes to the bare heights, and see!
> Where have you not been lain with?
> By the waysides you have sat awaiting lovers
>   like an Arab in the wilderness.
> You have polluted the land
>   with your vile harlotry. (Jer. 3:2)

And Ezekiel in the sixth century:

> For thus says [. . .] Yahweh: [I deal] with you, as you have done by despising the oath, and breaking [my] covenant. But I for my part will remember my covenant with you in the days of your youth and will establish an eternal covenant with you. And you will remember your ways and be ashamed, when I take both your elder and your younger sisters and give them to you as daughters, but not on account of your covenant. Yea, I will establish my covenant with you, and you shall know that I am Yahweh, so that you may remember it and be ashamed and never open your mouth again for shame, when I make atonement for you in all that you have done, says [. . .] Yahweh.[9]

But The Song of Songs follows a different line. It is an exception by using sexual imagery in a way quite other than the prophets did. It is an exposition of Genesis 2 in a positive way—it shows the goal of which Genesis is the origin. Its love songs are an exposition of the capacity for encounter between persons which results in a relationship which is whole ("saved"). It takes the language of sexual relationship, used in Genesis 2 to describe the internal basis of the covenant, to give an exposition of the covenant at work, the coming together of what was separated, the escape from solitariness and the arrival at communion, the personal realization of intimacy, an intimacy frustrated by sin but made possible by salvation.

> A comparison of Gen. 2 and the Song of Songs does at least reveal that what interested the authors of the creation saga and these love songs was the fact that in the relationship between man and woman —even prior to its character as the basis of the father-mother-child relationship—we have to do primarily with the question of an incomparable covenant, of an irresistibly purposed and effected union. The Song of Songs is one long description of the rapture, the unquenchable yearning and the restless willingness and readiness, with which both partners in this covenant hasten towards an encounter. Gen. 2 is even more radical in its great brevity. It tells us that only male and female together are man. The man alone is not yet man, for it is not good for him to be alone; nor can the female alone be man, for she is taken out of the man: "They twain shall be one flesh." Hence Gen. 2 speaks of the covenant made and irrevocably sealed. It sets at the beginning that which in the Song of Songs is the goal. It was for the sake of this covenant that God first created man as male and female. And the Song of Songs agrees. With this covenant in view, man and woman must and may and will hasten toward an encounter in spite of any hindrance and restriction.[10]

It is appropriate, then, that the Song of Songs, especially as it is used in the traditions of Passover, provide the stimulus and guide for the pastoral work of developing relationships which are derivative from the event of salvation, and which become in themselves instances of salvation. Covenant, the structure which God uses in his work, requires that people live in relationship if they are going to live in terms of their creation and salvation. Since all creation and all salvation are relational (covenantal), the life that grows and develops from that base and in that environment also must be relational (covenantal). For such reasons it is important to immerse pastoral .work in The Song of Songs, a *tour de force* in the business of personal relationships, and so provide a familiarity with the putative consequences of creation, via salvation. Genesis 2 plus Exodus 15 equals The Song of Songs.

Sexuality

The most striking feature of The Song of Songs is its eroticism: it is a collection of romantic love lyrics in which sexuality is pervasive and explicit. It is so striking that some readers see nothing else. Wesley Fuerst, for instance, writes of "the erotic language and exclusively sexual interest and content of the Song."[11] Theophile Meek is unequivocal: ". . . it is purely secular in character, with no apparent theological, religious, or moral attributes. God never once appears in it."[12]

But if the most striking feature to certain modern exegetes of the Song is its eroticism, the most striking feature in the history of its interpretation is its devotionalism. "Romantic love has always sought mystical sensations in the Song of Songs."[13] For as far back as we have any evidence, both Jews and Christians have read it as a description of the devotional life—the life of meditation and prayer. Rabbi Akiba said, " 'For all the world is not as worthy as the day on which the Song of Songs was given to Israel, for all the writings are holy, but the Song of Songs is the Holy of Holies.' "[14] Professor Meek calls it purely secular; Rabbi Akiba calls it " 'the Holy of Holies' "; who is right? Origen's twelve-volume commentary set the pattern for allegorical interpretation and was followed by most interpreters up to modern times. Bernard of Clairvaux preached eighty-six sermons on the Song and "got barely beyond the second chapter!"[15] There is variety in these expositions: some of them use allegory to give a historically connected reading of the history of the church, others use the language to describe the relation of God and the individual soul. For the most part, in these treatments there is no denial of the sexual nature of the language, only an insistence that the language reveals more than what took place in Northern Israel between two (or three) lovers; these commentaries discover in the Song a love description of the created relationships with which we all have to do.

The allegorical method of interpreting scripture is notoriously uncontrollable, and many excesses are indulged under its banner. But the modern decision to reject its interpretations, to avoid anything that is not explicitly cultic or absolutely secular, is heavy handed. As new evidence of early cultic practices in marriage, fertility rituals, and folk poetry has come to light in the last hundred years, scholars have scurried for explanations for the popularity of the Song and for its inclusion in Holy Scripture. The scholarship involved in such research is certainly sound, but most of it succumbs to what Erik Erikson warns against as the cult of "originology"—the belief that you have explained something when you have only located its origins and analyzed its elements.

In C. S. Lewis' *Voyage of the Dawn Treader* there is a conversational exchange between the children Eustace and Lucy who have just landed on a remote island and met Ramandu, a dazzling personage of wisdom. Lucy has just asked Ramandu about himself.

> "I am a star at rest, my daughter," answered Ramandu. . . .
> "In our world," said Eustace, "a star is a huge ball of flaming gas."
> "Even in your world, my son, that is not what a star is but only what it is made of."[16]

Likewise the Song. It is made of liturgical fragments from a fertility cult, wedding songs, love songs after the manner of the Arabic *wasif,* a rustic drama recounting the affairs of a youth with a country maiden—or whatever: these, though, are not what the Song is, but only what it is made of.

No book of the Bible has been served so badly by its modern interpreters (unless it is Revelation). They have made their way through the text like flat-footed Philistines. They have taken it apart and flattened it out in explanations that are about as interesting as a sex education chart in an eighth-grade hygiene class. They have assumed that the long centuries of the book's interpretation of allegorical, typological, and devotional expositions have been misguided—pious attempts to cover up explicit sexuality by a veneer of devotion. These assumptions, and they recur throughout the scholarly literature, are breezy arrogance. The ancients may not have known what the book was made of, but they knew what it was—an exposition of love in a creation in which all love in one way or another is an aspect of salvation.

The only context in which The Song of Songs is found is the canon of Holy Scripture. It had, no doubt, a pre-history of use by the community of faith previous to its admission to the canon, but the Song as we have it is embedded in scripture, which means that it has to do with God. And so even though the word "God" is not mentioned in the book even once, it is not a hermeneutical intrusion to posit a theological premise to the book. The common practice in the Christian church to use the language of romantic love in the Song as a way of understanding and developing a daily life of intimacy with God is not at all outlandish. All the intimacies possible to man and woman in love are an index to both the ecstasies and difficulties in our loving response to the God who loves us. "Human sexuality is the [*mimēsis*] of which divine love is the [*paradeigma*]."[17] Because it describes these intimacies with such exquisite accuracy, the Song has at various times in both Christian and Jewish history, been the most popular book in the Bible.

Philip Reiff has written:

> Mystics have never suspected that the worst is in the dark, as rationalists always have. Nor have they avoided the use of sexual imagery. On the contrary, even in the Christian tradition, erotic language was freely used to represent a vivid imagery of ways in which the inward man reverses the object of his interest and reaches out toward God. Mysticism bred acceptance of what the more ascetic rationalist tradition called the "animal" in man; mystics of all schools often decried the isolate and manipulative view of life bred by intellectualizing about it.[18]

"Sex and religion are intricately interwoven."[19] And they are interwoven because they are dealing with the basic elements of intimacy and the stuff of ecstasy. Modern scholars who have assumed that the reason that the church allegorically spiritualized The Song of Songs because she was prudish, simply don't understand the ancient mind, or the poetic mind for that matter, which is aware of the deep inner connections between the sexual and the spiritual. Before going to work at their exegetical desks they should recite Richard Wilbur's determination:

> "My eye will never know the dry disease
> Of thinking things no more than what he sees."[20]

Erich Auerbach has written an elaborate exposition of this biblical way of writing in his book *Mimesis,* and demonstrated how it has influenced so much Western literature. He wrote:

. . . an occurrence on earth signifies not only itself but at the same time another, which it predicts or confirms, without prejudice to the power of its concrete reality here and now. The connection between occurrences is not regarded as primarily a chronological or causal development but as a oneness within the divine plan, of which all occurrences are parts and reflections.[21]

It is what Melville, in *Moby Dick,* exclaims over in wonder as the "linked analogies—not the smallest atom stirs or lives on matter, but has its cunning duplicate in mind."[22]

This style of hermeneutic is much more true to the original than any historical-critical hermeneutic could ever be. For, as Gerard S. Sloyan has written:

The "primary literal sense" of a given passage which the modern age seeks so diligently is, in most cases, a poetic or symbolic sense. The Bible and the New Testament describe many things that happened in history. The events are in that sense historical. But history, so all-absorbing to the modern mind, is hardly what the Jewish and Christian writings are chiefly concerned with. They are interested in visible symbols of a God unseen.[23]

The context in which The Song of Songs comes to us is also the context for its interpretation, and that context is a story of covenant, the relationship between lover and beloved, in which the lover is God and the beloved is man, "male and female." The erotic content must be read in the theological context. The ancients did not read the Song devotionally because they were embarrassed by its sexuality, but because they understood sexuality in sacramental ways. Human love took its color from divine love. Reductive secular exegesis of the Song is an admission that our understanding of human love is unrelated to all that we have learned about God's love. If we read the sexual language of the Song in terms different from the divorce court, the popular play, and the glossy magazine, that may not be evidence that we are afraid of sex, but that we are bold with God.

Covenant

The Song of Songs "is the only book in the Bible to have all its content put into the mouth of speakers."[24] There are two main speakers: the maid from Shulem, and her rustic shepherd lover, plus assorted background voices from the watchmen and the maids of Jerusalem, after the manner of a Greek chorus. (Some interpreters posit a third main speaker in the person of King Solomon.) This literary feature leads to the insight that salvation expresses itself in love in the ambience of personal relationships. Salvation is not an intensification of the ego, the solitary soul deepening into mystical profundities, nor is it an abstraction from the self, an idealization of the personal into some fragment of feeling or thought. Salvation is a personal relationship which is nurtured by the Word which creates and by words which praise. The Song is thus representative of an environment in which all biblical faith operates—a world of dialogic speech, a world in which there are questions and answers, invitations and commitments, promises and fulfillments—a world in which words bring new reality into being. It is a world of persons who speak and listen, a world where lives intermingle, a world Charles Williams has described with the term *coinherence*.

This is enormously significant for all pastoral work that takes place in the form of personal conversations which have intimacy as their goal. The pastor is party to conversations in which he or she and others are seeking to overcome the barriers of division, coolness, or indifference—to get into the other, to discover the truth of the other, to probe the meaning of the other. Speech from the pulpit, or from behind the lectern, may be rhetorical and declamatory, but speech in the home and the study takes on other qualities. Pastoral conversations are conversations between persons who are seeking intimacy.

Paradigmatically, all pastoral conversation is a conversation between lovers. Those observers of pastoral life who have discerned a high degree of sexuality between pastor and people, have seen truly—but (at least in the analyses I have read) they have misinterpreted it badly. The sexuality is there because both pastor and people are sexual beings. And the sexuality is heightened in their relationships because there is a quest for intimacy—seeking ways in which the oneness created by God in Eden and redeemed in Exodus can be realized in the everyday lives in which they are "working out their salvation" with fear and trembling.

The main biblical word for this structure of relationship between a saving God and a saved people is covenant (*berit*). The word does not occur in the Song, but the Song is placed in the Bible in which the word *covenant* is definitive. Covenant, in effect, means that humanity cannot understand life apart from a defined and revealed relationship with God. Before anything else we are part of an arrangement—a relationship. And the relationship has to do with persons, with man "in the image of God" and with man "male and female" (Gen. 1:27), for "it is not good that man should be alone." (2:18)

The word *covenant* comes from the world of international politics. Archaelogical discoveries of treaty documents from the Hittites, the Assyrians, the Babylonians, the Egyptians, and the Canaanites, and other Near Eastern peoples have given a specific content to the word covenant that demonstrates how Israel, in detail, understood her life as lived out completely under conditions set by God. And so even though the word *covenant* does not appear in the Song, the Song is sung among a people who understood all of life in terms of covenant. Delbert Hillers says that "we are apt to miss much if we look only at those texts where the term 'covenant' itself occurs."[25] Particularly we will miss much if we fail to look at the Song. For the Song provides an instance of understanding and realizing the experience of covenant from the inside, using not the objective language of international treaty-making, but the subjective language of personal love-making. In this way it provides one of the most vivid, biblical expositions of the inner contents of covenant that we have.[26] In the explicit references to covenant in scripture the treaties define the conditions whereby nations can live in peace, and by extension, the people of God can live in righteousness; here in the Song it is otherwise—the well-known language of sexual love is used to describe the inner dynamics of all who seek to experience the personal realities of living out a whole, healthy, and fulfilled relationship with another. Just as the books of Moses tell the story of the making of covenant, so the Song sings the relationship that one realizes in covenant relationships.

The movement from the Song of Moses that celebrates God's act of salvation to the Song of Solomon that explores the subjective experience of that salvation (which corresponds to the transition from pastoral *preaching* to pastoral *prayer-conversation*) is abrupt: the first word in the Song (in Hebrew) is "Kiss me!" (*yiššaqeni*)—a direct, and passionate, appeal for intimacy. This person does not want to talk about theology, does not want to gossip about love, does not want to get on a committee to do something for God. There is no time for cultural "platonic" conversation, no use for that which in the theological world goes under the label of "apologetics." The lonely isolation of the solitary person must be invaded. Life, to be meaningful, must be joined: intimacy is a requirement of wholeness.

Pastoral work is familiar with the demand, if not so familiar with its bold expression (for not many know what they need so clearly, or are so bold to express it directly). All those who have heard the word of salvation and have responded to it in faith are on the way to realizing its implications in their daily lives. The desire is expressed either openly or circuitously. It may or may not be expressed to the pastor, but it is always expressed somehow or other in the community in which the pastor works. We are trained to have ears to hear the inarticulate "Kiss me!" that is hidden under all kinds of other demands and requests.

The maiden is clear in her supporting reason, "for your love is better than wine." The stock meaning of *wine*, in this context, is conviviality. It lifts a person from isolation into shared fellowship. For those who are dwelling overmuch on their own selves, nurturing feelings of inadequacy and guilt, wine, temporarily, can free them from such inwardness and liberate them to talk freely, speech being an act of community. And when I talk, even if it is about myself, I am acknowledging the presence (and importance) of another. Wine is praised because it releases inhibitions and stimulates conversation, that is, banishes isolation and bridges the chasms that separate individuals. But "love is better than wine," because love does it better —it joins the *Thou* and the *I*. It dissolves the separating wall and engenders the communication of emotion, thought, and purpose.

And that, of course, is why most people are in church. Most of them have tried "wine," and are dissatisfied with it—not that it doesn't work for a while, but they are looking for something that works permanently (eternally). Pastors are far too condescending towards their parishioners. We do not credit them with previous choices (very frequently made on an unconscious level, to be sure, but made nevertheless) that have rejected the pseudo and partial intimacies of the world in order to be open to the intimacies of salvation. Assuming they don't know the difference, we offer them community projects, committee assignments, a job in the Women's Association, or a place on the bowling team. And they, thinking that we know what we are doing, follow our suggestions—"and are not fed." "Love is better than wine." But committees aren't; liturgical innovations aren't; entertainment isn't; counseling techniques accredited by the American Counseling Association aren't.

The third verse of the Song is: "Your anointing oils are fragrant, your name is oil poured out; therefore the maidens love you." The factual statement, "your anointing oils are fragrant," precipitates a poetic fantasy, "your name is oil poured out." Oils applied to the body give it fragrance and augment its sensory pleasures. In addition to the pleasures of seeing and feeling, smelling is added to the pleasures of the beloved's body. This rather commonplace experience with perfumes and anointing oils sets off a more subtle reflection on the analogous sensory response to the name of the beloved: "your name is oil poured out." Audition is also a sensory experience. The *name* of the other, representing his or her very being in sound, affects the ears like oil does the nostrils.

The sensory possibilities of sound are enormous and much more deeply appreciated in ancient and primitive cultures than in our own technological cities. Overwhelmed by noise we are not so sensitive to the pleasures of sound as was ancient humanity. Still we are not without experience or susceptibility—especially when the sound is the sound of our own name. In the Hebrew text there is a word play on the words "name" and "oil" which in Hebrew are *shemen* and *shem* (using the LXX variant). The words predominate in soft sibilants and labials. *Shemen* and *shem* sound alike just as they function alike by evoking by sensory means (smell and sound) the actual physical presence of the other. For it is not *any* sound but the sound of the personal name which is important. Intimacy is not a vague mystic merging into the world-soul; it is a personal and particular joining with a specific other: Adam with Eve, "Solomon" with the

Shulammite. Intimacy is not an abstraction but a personalization. And persons have names. This is why the Bible has so much to do with names, both of persons and of God, for the name gives specific, historical, concrete meaning to what is being done in salvation. As Barth put it: "To be God's partner in this covenant, man himself needed a partner."[27]

And so pastoral work is a concentration on names. After the Bible, the church roll is the most important book in a pastor's study. We work in communities which are composed of names. The pastor (like Adam in the garden) gives names—presents a person by name at the baptismal font, invokes the name of God at the table, proclaims the name of God from the pulpit, and combines those names in every pastoral conversation and prayer. To become familiar with the name of the other, and to find that the other is familiar with one's name is the stuff of intimacy. Without names there can be no pastoral work, for, as Rosenstock-Huessy writes, "As long as we are only taught and addressed in the mass, our name never falls upon us as the power that dresses our wounds, lifts our hearts, and makes us rise and walk."[28]

The second aspect of covenant that is elaborated in the Song is the difficulty of intimacy. Intimacy is not easily achieved. Even though the structure providing for intimacy (the covenant) is sure, in the living of it there are hindrances and interferences. The person who responds to the saving event of God in Christ does not feel continuously and without the disturbances of doubt oneness with God, although he or she knows in fact that all sins are forgiven. These difficulties are expressed in several passages in the Song, most notably in 3:1–4:

> Upon my bed by night
>   I sought him whom my soul loves;
> I sought him, but found him not;
>   I called him, but he gave no answer.
> "I will rise now and go about the city,
>   in the streets and in the squares;
> I will seek him whom my soul loves."
>   I sought him, but found him not.
> The watchmen found me,
>   as they went about in the city.

> "Have you seen him whom my soul loves?"
> Scarcely had I passed them,
>   when I found him whom my soul loves.
> I held him, and would not let him go
>   until I had brought him into my mother's house,
>   and into the chamber of her that conceived me.

The accounts of saints who tell of the "dark nights" of the soul are familiar. Their search for God seems endless and futile, but is broken into by moments of ecstasy when they find (or are found by) the one they sought. This longing and frustration are clearly understood by persons in love. For the beloved is a mystery: there is otherness that we can never completely fathom or chart. We search for the clue, we ask questions of the "watchmen." But we don't know. The coming together of two uniquely created persons is not instinctual and automatic as in the coupling of animals. Sex is not only the means for the reproduction of the species—it is an aspect of *knowing* (the biblical word for sexual intercourse). Where there is knowing, there is previously that which is not known: areas of ignorance and mystery in both body and spirit.

There are recurrent elements of quest in the life of the spirit: there is longing and there is search.

> Whither has your beloved gone,
>   O fairest among women? (6:1)

But the longing is not meandering, nor the search fumbling—there is direction and there is goal:

> My beloved has gone down to his garden
>   to the beds of spices,
> to pasture his flock in the gardens,
>   and to gather lilies. (6:2)

If he or she is not with me at the moment, if I do not feel his or her touch, or experience his or her presence, I know that the absence is for my good, and that there will be reunion which I will enjoy. The appetites that God has created in us lead to the satisfactions he has promised.

Pastoral work acknowledges the difficulty and the pain of the quest and shares it. It does not attribute the agony of longing to a neurosis, it does not search for a cause in moral deficiency, it does not try to "cure" it by working for an adaptive adjustment to "reality." It honors the quest. The difficult painful moments of unfulfilled longing are integral to the nature of the relationships.

It is not the pastor's job to simplify the spiritual life, to devise common-denominator formulas, to smooth out the path of discipleship. Some difficulties are inherent in the way of spiritual growth—to deny them, to minimize them, or to offer shortcuts is to divert the person from true growth. It is the pastor's task, rather, to be companion to persons who are in the midst of difficulty, to acknowledge the difficulty and thereby give it significance, and to converse and pray with them through the time so that the loneliness is lightened, somewhat, and hope is maintained, somehow.

The simplifiers, however well-intentioned they are, are the bane of good pastoral work. The spate of inspirational-testimonial religious writing that seems to find such a ready market in the Christian community is an instance of such well-intentioned simplification that results in later complications. The stories are not honest. They are written under the direction of a market-oriented editor, not to tell the truth of Christian conversion and growth, but to tell the one part of the truth that will appeal to the element of spiritual sloth in every Christian that wants to skip the hard parts of discipleship. Such books are reminiscent of the self-confessed method of Liberace, perhaps the most popular pianist in the world, as a musician. "My whole trick," he says, "is to keep the tune well out in front. If I play Tschaikovsky, I play his melodies and skip his spiritual struggles. Naturally I condense. I have to know just how many notes my audience will stand for. If there's time left over, I fill in with a lot of runs up and down the keyboard."[29]

Persons who read these wonderful stories in which everything works out so smoothly and with such grand results, conclude that they must be going about the Christian faith all wrong, since they still have many nights when "I sought him, but found him not," and experience episodes in which they go about the city streets asking the bewildered question, "Have you seen him whom my soul loves?" They read these simplified versions of spiritual accomplishment, with all the dark nights left out and all the unanswered questions excised, and are sure that they have gotten off the track somehow. They come to the pastor and say, "I guess I'm not a Christian after all." But the Bible does not tell the story of Christian pilgrimage in such ways. In the Bible, even in moments of clear and ecstatic revelation, "some doubted." (Matt. 28:17)

A second passage has similar features, but there is a difference in that the conclusion is not ecstasy, but pain:

> I slept, but my heart was awake.
> Hark! my beloved is knocking.
> "Open to me, my sister, my love,
>   my dove, my perfect one;
> for my head is wet with dew,
>   my locks with the drops of the night."
> I had put off my garment,
>   how could I put it on?
> I had bathed my feet,
>   how could I soil them?
> My beloved put his hand to the latch,
>   and my heart was thrilled within me.
> I arose to open to my beloved,
>   and my hands dripped with myrrh,
> my fingers with liquid myrrh,
>   upon the handles of the bolt.
> I opened to my beloved,
>   but my beloved had turned and gone.
> My soul failed me when he spoke.
> I sought him, but found him not;
>   I called him, but he gave no answer.
> The watchmen found me,
>   as they went about in the city;
> they beat me, they wounded me,
>   they took away my mantle,
>   those watchmen of the walls. (5:2–7)

In this passage the beloved is sought by the lover, but having already retired to bed for the night, is slow to respond. She wants her lover, but, after all, she has already disrobed and washed. Getting up would mean putting on clothes and getting her feet dirty again, making it necessary to repeat the whole routine of getting ready for bed. So she procrastinates. She delays. When she finally does get to the door, she finds her lover is gone. Panicked, she goes to look for him, calling and running through the streets. The watchmen find her and beat her, presumably for disturbing the peace in the night hours, and take away her coat so she will have to go home again to get warm.

This world is no friend to grace. Seeking for intimacy at any level —with God or with persons—is not a venture that gets the support of many people. Intimacy is not good for business. It is inefficient, it lacks "glamour." If love of God can be reduced to a ritualized hour of worship, if love of another can be reduced to an act of sexual intercourse, then routines are simple and the world can be run efficiently. But if we will not settle for the reduction of love to lust and of faith to ritual, and run through the streets asking for more, we will most certainly disturb the peace and be told to behave ourselves and go back to the homes and churches where we belong. If we refuse to join the cult of exhibitionists who do a soul striptease on cue, or the "flashers" who expose their psychic nudity as a diversion from long-term covenental intimacy, we are dismissed as hopeless puritans. Intimacy is no easy achievement. There is pain— longing, disappointment, and hurt. But if the costs are considerable, the rewards are magnificent, for in relationship with another and with the God who loves us we complete the humanity for which we were created. We stutter and stumble, wander and digress, delay and procrastinate; but we do learn to love even as we are loved, steadily and eternally, in Jesus Christ.

The pastoral implications of these passages are extensive, for every person in every parish is involved in the desires and the difficulties of intimacy. They experience them when they sit down to breakfast with other members of the family; they experience them when they go to work with other persons in the factory or business or shop; they experience them when they go to bed with a spouse; they experience them when they sit in a classroom in school or university. In every encounter there is the desire for closeness—the need to break through the defenses of sin, the need to be in touch with another. But there are also difficulties: some of these derive from within from sheer laziness:

> I had bathed my feet,
>   how could I soil them? (5:3)

Some difficulties come from deeply embedded neurotic responses that inhibit or prevent open relationships:

> Do not gaze at me because I am swarthy,
>   because the sun has scorched me. (1:6)

And some difficulties are imposed by others:

> they beat me, they wounded me,
>   they took away my mantle. (5:7)

The difficulties are of different sorts and cannot be dealt with by formulae or by generalizations; they require the personal, individual attention of pastoral conversation and prayer.

Three times in the Song there is the plea:

> I adjure you, O daughters of Jerusalem,
> . . . .
> that you stir not up nor awaken love
>   until it please. (2:7, 3:5, 8:4)

Intimacy is, in both love and faith, full of tensions. When fulfillment is delayed, desire is bitter. Between falling in love and consummating love, between the promise and the fulfillment, between the boundaries, that is, that are defined by covenant, it is the task of persevering and patient prayer to keep love ardent and faith zealous.

Which is why prayer is the chief pastoral work in relation to a person's desires for and difficulties with intimacy. Anything less or other than prayer fails to deal with either the ultimacy of the desires or the complexity of the difficulties. Prayer with and for persons centers the desire in God and puts the difficulties in perspective under God. Prayer is thus the language, *par excellence,* of the covenant: it is quintessential pastoral conversation that takes seriously the relationships that matter most, both human and divine. In prayer the desires are not talked about, they are expressed to God. In prayer the difficulties are not analyzed and studied, they are worked through with God. If the goal is intimacy, it will not be arrived at by teaching or counsel or therapy (although any of these ministries may provide assistance) but by dealing personally with those who count, with Creator and creature.

Body

"I cannot help thinking," said General Gordon, "that the body has much to do with religion."[30] Which is no more than to say that religion, the Christian religion at any rate, is sacramental: the visible is evidence of the invisible, the profane is the conduit for the sacred, the physical is a container for the spiritual. The biblical sacraments of baptism and eucharist, in which water is a sacrament of forgiveness and food a sacrament of eternal life, are instances of what occurs throughout the created order. Moreover, since God chose to use a physical body as a means of revealing his saving love to us ("And the Word became flesh and dwelt among us, full of grace and truth, we have beheld his glory . . ." John 1:14), it is well within the biblical boundaries to use the Song's keen interest in the body as a means for understanding aspects of intimacy with God. Wordsworth's lines could very well serve as subtitle to the Song of Songs,

". . . the human form
To me became an index of delight,
Of grace and honour, power and worthiness."[31]

An index is a listing of items which receive fuller treatment in another place. The "index" of the body is a listing of reality which receives its fullest treatment in the incarnation, for the body is never just a body but a region of being, a network of living processes combining creation and salvation. Since the Song dwells leisurely and longingly on various bodily features, particularly those parts evocative of sexual relationship, it is natural (or supernatural) to use these erotic meditations sacramentally, that is, as analogies by which we understand God through the expressions in which we experience intimacy with others. In such ways sex becomes a parable for prayer, prayer being the inner quest for intimacy with God of which sex is the bodily expression with persons.

There are four passages in the Song which predominate in describing the body of the beloved: 4:1–15; 5:10–16; 6:4–10; 6:13b —7:9. This form of poetry is termed *wasif,* after the Arabic (literally "description"). The *wasif* was very likely used in ancient times as part of a wedding ritual, in which the bride danced before assembled guests, and they, in turn, sang her beauty. The last passage will be used here as being characteristic.

> Why should you look upon the Shulammite,
>   as upon a dance before two armies?
>
> How graceful are your feet in sandals,
>   O queenly maiden!
> Your rounded thighs are like jewels,
>   the work of a master hand.
> Your navel is a rounded bowl
>   That never lacks mixed wine.
> Your belly is a heap of wheat,
>   encircled with lilies.
> Your two breasts are like two fawns,
>   twins of a gazelle.
> Your neck is like an ivory tower.
> Your eyes are pools in Heshbon,
>   by the gate of Bathrabbim.
> Your nose is like a tower of Lebanon,
>   overlooking Damascus.
> Your head crowns you like Carmel,
>   and your flowing locks are like purple;
>   a king is held captive in the tresses.
>
> How fair and pleasant you are,
>   O loved one, delectable maiden!
> You are stately as a palm tree,
>   and your breasts are like its clusters.
> I say I will climb the palm tree
>   and lay hold of its branches.
> Oh, may your breasts be like clusters of the vine,
>   and the scent of your breath like apples,
> and your kisses like the best wine
>   that goes down smoothly,
>   gliding over lips and teeth.

Bodily delight is evoked through the medium of the dance (6:13b). Among the Hebrews, dance was a form of worship. The ritual movements of the dance put the entire body at the service of spirit, expressing adoration, joy, and enthusiasm to the God who creates and redeems the body. Miriam's maidens danced their way out of the Red Sea, illustrating with their bodies the song of salvation (Exod. 15:20–21). David danced before the ark as it was brought up in procession to Jerusalem (2 Sam. 14:15), expressing physical delight in the God who comes near in salvation. Dance is a way of prayer, the body put to the means of adoration, mind and muscle coordinated to the glory of God.

Following the reference to the dance, every metaphor and simile for the body is plundered for images which will express adoration (7:1–9). The description proceeds from feet to head, dwelling erotically on each part. The body of the beloved centers existence, each part making connection with something else. The body is an index. Persons in love and persons who pray, all, that is, who use language for the purposes of intimacy and relationship, speak thus. For the beauties of the other are, finally, beyond the capacities of speech: awe, reverence, desire, and gratitude stretch language to its limits.

Both prayer and sex have to do with Another who is in some ways the same and yet in significant ways different from me:

> . . . man needs a being like him and yet different from him, so that in it he will recognize himself but not only himself, since it is to him a Thou as truly as he is an I. It is in this way that God Himself will confront man, having intercourse and dealings with him.[32]

There is an earlier sequence in the Song in which the self-deprecating "I am [only] a rose of Sharon" is quickly and ingeniously turned by the lover into a celebrative compliment: You are ". . . a lily among brambles." (2:1–2) This same extravagant inventiveness is at work in the *wasf.* One gets the impression that there is nothing in the beloved's body that cannot be praised if only the right image can be found:

> Your teeth are like a flock of shorn ewes
>   that have come up from the washing,
> all of which bear twins,
>   and not one among them is bereaved. (4:2)

> "Who is this that looks forth like the dawn,
>   fair as the moon, bright as the sun,
>   terrible as an army with banners?" (6:10)

Adoration, ennoblement, single-mindedness—all the things that we experience when we "fall in love"—are evidence of what happens when we are loved/saved. Love changes everything for and in us—our ideas about ourselves, our attitudes toward others, our values and our goals. By analogy, the impact of God's love makes our life *mean* something ultimately, makes it *good* for something, eternally.

Pastoral work is a ministry for taking seriously the details which differentiate us from each other and from God, and then praising them, for " 'In separateness only does love learn definition.' "[33] By listening attentively to a person's dreams, desires, and longings, and by sharing passionately a person's struggles, painful frustrations, and difficulties, significance is given to them. The differences become thereby not neurotic annoyances but items in the experience of salvation. By immersing himself or herself in the relational details of a people, the pastor makes an index of prayers for them. Sherwood Anderson speaks someplace of "the terrible importance of the flesh in human relations."[34] The actual details of intimate needs and relational realities become the stuff of prayer. Desires are shaped into adoration and difficulties are formed into petitions.

There is no clear line separating the conversations that a pastor has with people and the continuation of those conversations in prayer. The single most significant phrase that a pastor can speak (either aloud or *sub voce*) is "I will pray for you." It means that the conversation in which they have just been engaged will be continued with God as partner to the conversation. Much of such pastoral work is hidden and secret. Because of its intimate qualities it must be thus. (Again, sexual analogies are clear.) Pastors should not pray aloud with everyone they meet and should not say, "I'll pray for you" to everyone who announces a problem. But we must pray *for* everyone we meet. Before, after, and during conversations prayer must be made, for how else will a pastor work at the center as intercessor before God on behalf of the deep desires and the persistent difficulties which concentrate their force in each person?

There is one other aspect of the *wasif* that is suggestive for pastoral work in relation to prayer, and that is its leisurely quality. These sequences *linger* over each detail. Dalliance is the atmosphere proper to both lovemaking and prayer. Edward Dahlberg's counsel regarding *Walden* fits the mood of the *wasif* " '[it] cannot be rushed into men's hearts . . . *persuade and hint.*' "[35] Intimacy will not yield to rapacious assault.

Above all, this is no work for what has been apotheosized by our compulsive society as the "busy pastor." A sense of hurry in pastoral work disqualifies one for the work of conversation and prayer which develops relationships which meet personal needs. There are heavy demands put upon pastoral work, true; there is difficult work to be engaged in, yes. But the pastor must not be "busy." Busyness is an illness of spirit, a rush from one thing to another because there is no ballast of vocational integrity and no confidence in the primacy of grace. In order for there to be conversation and prayer which do the pastoral work of meeting the intimacy needs among people, there must be a wide margin of quiet leisure which defies the functional, technological, dehumanizing definitions that are imposed upon people by others in the community. Henri Nouwen writes:

> Without the solitude of heart, our relationships with others easily become needy and greedy, sticky and clinging, dependent and sentimental, exploitative and parasitic, because without the solitude of heart we cannot experience the others as different from ourselves but only as people who can be used for the fulfillment of our own, often hidden, needs.[36]

Eucharist

The associations that are set up by placing the Song of Songs in the context of Passover worship develop further correspondences in relation to the Eucharist, the Christian act of worship which owes so much to Passover. In suggesting these correspondences it is not necessary to decide beforehand whether the Eucharist was instituted as a replacement for (and fulfillment of) the Passover ritual (as the Synoptic accounts have it) or as a separate act which draws its symbolism and timing from the Passover event (as John describes it): in either case the Passover background is undisputed and insures liturgical and pastoral continuities for the worshiping people of God.

The Eucharist, like Passover, is the act of worship which remembers the decisive act of salvation, enacts the event in a ritual meal in which participation by the people demonstrates a faith involvement in God's action, and looks forward to a complete and final consummation. In the Johannine account, the Passover event was preceded by a lengthy conversation and prayer in which various details of what it means to live in daily, ongoing intimacy with the Lord of salvation are elaborated first in discussion and discourse (chapters 14–16) and finally in prayer (chapter 17). Both the conversation and the prayer are clearly pastoral, showing a similarity in function, if not in form and content, that the Song served in relation to the Passover meal, and so inviting an exploration of the ways in which salvation works between the acts of worship, "between Sundays." In summary, both the Song and the Johannine discourse/prayer provide guidance to "Continue steadfastly in prayer, being watchful in it with thanksgiving." (Col. 4:2)

The Eucharist is a particularly important pastoral focus for the concerns that are represented by the Song, because it combines the emphases of the institutional, the mystical, and the individual—any one of which, separated from the others, becomes something either bizarre or unlovely. It is one of the pastor's tasks to keep those parts together. The unity is represented in the celebration of the Eucharist, for it is at the Lord's Table that the connection is maintained between an irreducible core of historical data, a faith in the presence of a living Lord, and the inner responses of personal prayer.

Under the influence of the Eucharistic Table the Song continues to yield up insights, as it has in the context of Passover. Out of an environment of celebrated salvation pastoral work in the form of prayer develops that which is responsive to the needs of and for intimacy.

Thomas Aquinas held that the meaning of all pastoral care was "to prepare the Christian people for the celebration of the Eucharist."[37] But pastoral work is just as much a derivation from the Eucharist as preparation for it, for it helps those who have received into their bodies and spirits the life of Christ to realize that love in every detail of every relationship. The prayers offered at the Eucharistic Table are continued in homes and hospitals, in committee rooms and at work tables. Pastoral work gives visibility to these continuities.

There are three aspects of pastoral prayer that have their roots in the Eucharist, to which the Song is useful in giving imaginative shape. Used this way, the Song functions not as ". . . a model to be imitated; it is a parent, begetting offspring at once like and unlike itself, and each new child has his individual traits as well as his family likeness."[38]

In the first instance the Song establishes pastoral prayer in an atmosphere redolent with celebration, thus continuing the eucharistic joy ("this is the joyful feast of the people of God") into the routines of daily intercession.

> I compare you, my love,
>   to a mare of Pharaoh's chariots.
> Your cheeks are comely with ornaments,
>   your neck with strings of jewels.
> We will make you ornaments of gold,
>   studded with silver. (1.9–11)

God, delighting in us, festoons his creatures, just as we, when we delight in another, enhance and elaborate the beloved. With the help of a vocabulary learned in the Song we see God's people (and ourselves) not through the dirty lens of our own muddled feelings, and not through the smudgy window of another's carping criticism, but in terms of God's word. We never know how good we can look, how delightful we can feel, or how strong we can be until we hear ourselves addressed in love by God or by the one who represents God's love to us. *"That which in itself is without value acquires value by the fact that it is the object of God's love."*[39] A large percentage of persons who are in the care of a pastor are burdened with feelings of inadequacy and are without conscious self-worth. How is the pastor to reassure them? How rebuild a sense of worth in them? How else than by extending the lines of eucharistic joy in prayer. Not that prayer is a quick cure or an instant therapy, for it is a lifelong work; but it has the advantage of actually starting at the center instead of puttering at the edges.

In this regard the most important thing a pastor can do for a person is to be grateful to God for that particular person: celebrate with joy the sheer existence of this particular instance of God's creation without regard to moral quality or spiritual maturity. Prayer which is conceived by the Spirit via the Song will have this happy character because it will see the person in the environment of the covenant, and therefore in the way of salvation. The practice of such prayer will also prevent what Bonhoeffer sternly warns against, that

"A pastor should not complain about his congregation, certainly never to other people, but also not to God. A congregation has not been entrusted to him in order that he should become its accuser before God and men."[40]

Apart from prayer the beauty and worth in another is not always obvious, for pastoral sight is frequently astigmatic with sin. But what we call ugliness is only matter that is out of place or out of balance. When the pastor prays with and for another, the proportions change and new perceptions are formed.

> Behold, you are beautiful, my love;
>   behold, you are beautiful;
>   your eyes are doves.
> Behold, you are beautiful, my beloved,
>   truly lovely. (1:15–16)

Such prayers perceive possibilities far better than we can calculate on the basis of our most sober pastoral evaluations and judgments:

> What is that coming up from the wilderness,
>   like a column of smoke,
> perfumed with myrrh and frankincense,
>   with all the fragrant powders of the merchant?
> Behold, it is the litter of Solomon! (3:6–7)

Solomon—the best of lovers! The eucharistic instinct for wholeness, for being satisfied with nothing but the best, is confirmed in the work of prayer. Coventry Patmore wrote, "If we would find in God that full satisfaction of all our desires which He promises, we must believe extravagantly . . ."[41] The hyperbolic joy expressed in the Song does not divert prayer into fantasy as might be feared, but deepens it into true biblical wonder.

> Many waters cannot quench love,
>   neither can floods drown it. (8:7)

Not indifference, not doubt, not guilt, can put out the fire of God's love in and for us. His love will burn deep into our lives, penetrating habits and dreams until it ascends into flames of joyous adoration.

A second strand of pastoral prayer that has its origin in the Eucharist and is encouraged by the Song is a passionate involvement in the action of redemption and reconciliation—"poured out for many for the forgiveness of sins." (Matt. 26:28) Such prayer denies the pastor the bystander role of an impersonal historian, an observer who explains and advises others, and leads into the way of an adventurous participation in the way of righteousness. Pastors are not archaeologists, digging through the rubble of sin, identifying layers of conflict, assigning labels of blame and guilt; we are contestants.

> He brought me to the banqueting house,
>   and his banner over me was love. (2:4)

A raised banner marks a place where battle is joined; it also marks a site of victory. When the banner is love, both conflict and consummation in our everyday affairs are parables of God's victorious relations with us. God's love is an assault on our indifference and a victory over our rebellion. Pastoral prayer shares and participates in his untiring grace and unrelenting purpose to complete the work of love in his people. Such Song-nurtured prayers pulse with the drama of reconciliation:

> "Arise, my love, my fair one,
>   and come away;
> for lo, the winter is past,
>   the rain is over and gone.
> The flowers appear on the earth,
>   the time of singing has come,
> and the voice of the turtledove
>   is heard in our land.
> The fig tree puts forth its figs,
>   and the vines are in blossom;
>   they give forth fragrance.
> Arise, my love, my fair one,
>   and come away." (2:10–13)

Prayers do not calculate their chances by evaluating a person's past; they are awakened to action by the word of promise. Christ's love brings fresh vigor to lives as it announces the springtime of resurrection. Prayer is the place where chill doubts which result from disappointment and failure are dispelled and a warm faith in resurrection love is created.

The pastor at prayer is not passive or detached but active and committed. The language of sexual passion put to the use of prayer shows the intensity, the almost violence, which goes into whole and intimate relationships:

> turn, my beloved, be like a gazelle,
>   or a young stag upon rugged mountains. (2:17)

For there is always a danger that pastoral professionalism will harden into ecclesiastical impersonalism. But the Song arouses passionate response, putting adrenalin into prayer so that the desires expressed in it flow through the intercessory Christ and satisfy longings and provide fulfillments. The famous inversion in the Song—"My beloved is mine and I am his" (2:16) "I am my beloved's and my beloved is mine" (6:3)—exhibits the end-product of prayers that develop out of the eucharistic action.

A third strand of pastoral prayer that is rooted in the Eucharist is a strong sense of expectation ("until he comes" 1 Cor. 11:26). Here again the Song gives both impetus and images to pray in hope for those who have, by faith, received our Lord and who are therefore in a position to be moved by His Spirit:

> Awake, O north wind,
>   and come, O south wind!
> Blow upon my garden. (4:16)

We can do nothing until we are set in motion by God's spirit ("wind" and "spirit" are the same word in the biblical languages). Love is latent until stirred into motion by God; virtue is dormant until awakened to responsive obedience by God. How many persons leave the act of worship still asleep? The Spirit, praying in us, is a counterforce to the skeptics who see people walk out of church little different from when they entered. The pastor who strives to nurture intimacy with God and others is met with puzzled questions: "What is your beloved more than another beloved?" (5:9) Which is to say, "Why make such a fuss about such unpractical things? Why not get where the action is?" But the soaring intimacies of love and faith only make sense to those who participate in them. Bystanders don't see what all the commotion is about. Their comments are uncomprehending. It is pastoral prayer that keeps, in such an atmosphere, steadfast hope and maintains a pressure for growth in faith, defiant of the "cultured despisers."

These prayers are a form of dreaming that shapes the future. Dreams are important for they organize the present and direct its energies to future fulfillments. Thoreau's idea that the dreams of youth fashion a habitation to which the work of adulthood makes a staircase, says a great deal about prayers which take the eucharistic words as stuff for fashioning daily participation in the kingdom of God.

> I went down to the nut orchard,
>   to look at the blossoms of the valley,
> to see whether the vines had budded,
>   whether the pomegranates were in bloom.
> Before I was aware, my fancy set me
>   in a chariot beside my prince. (6:11–12)

Just as the blossoms and buds in the nut orchard, while not yet the fruit, are a sign and promise of it to the day-dreaming maiden, and precipitate the fancy that all will be fulfilled in days to come "in a chariot beside my prince," so in the quietness of prayer and the solitude of dreaming meditation realizes the end of what God has begun and grasps by faith the complete work in which we shall "know even as we are known."

But if expectant prayer is a form of dreaming, it is not "dreamy." There is urgency in it. When things have to do with basic needs for love and for God, we will not be put off. The final words of the Song are impatient of delay and passionate in anticipation:

> Make haste, my beloved,
>   and be like a gazelle
> or a young stag
>   upon the mountains of spices. (8:14)

This is equivalent to the New Testament church's cry: "Our Lord, come!" (2 Cor. 16:22) Maranatha!, and to the closing words of the Apocalypse, "The Spirit and the Bride say, 'Come.' And let him who hears say, 'Come.' And let him who is thirsty come, let him who desires take the water of life without price." (Rev. 22:17) The language of prayer is always, in some degree, urgent; now is the day.

Pastors will communicate this best not by raising their voices in rhetorical declamations but by immersing themselves in the prayers of the biblical revelation which are permeated by excitement and urgency:

> When I think of thy ways,
> . . . .
> I hasten and do not delay. (Ps. 119:59–60)

Prayer is the pastoral work that is most suited for recognizing the compelling quality of God's invitations and promises, and perpetuating it in others.

The
PASTORAL WORK
of
STORY-MAKING:
RUTH

It is not an abstraction called Humanity that is to be saved. It is you, . . . your soul, and, in some sense yet to be understood, even your body, that was made for the high and holy place. All that you are . . . every fold and crease of your individuality was devised from all eternity to fit God as a glove fits a hand. All that intimate particularity which you can hardly grasp yourself, much less communicate to your fellow creatures, is no mystery to Him. He made those ins and outs that He might fill them. Then He gave your soul so curious a life because it is the key designed to unlock that door, of all the myriad doors in Him.

—C. S. Lewis[1]

Every week the pastor makes a fairly short but exceedingly painful journey from the chancel to the narthex. In the chancel everything has been ordered and poised: the scriptures have told the plain story of salvation; the sermon has retold the story in the idiom of the assembled people; the hymns have gathered the voices of worshipers into prayers and praises that establish continuity with God's people in every time and place; actions at Table and Font have set forth God's grace and providence as real and available for every person present; prayers have created encounter with a personal God.

Each Lord's Day worship divides the waters of chaos which on command roll back to the right and to the left while the people march through in glad triumph. For an hour all truth is proportioned, contemporary, and complete. God's word is proclaimed, affirmed, and accepted. Then the pastor lifts his arms in benediction, giving witness to the wholeness of salvation and promising the continuities of blessing through the week. He goes to the narthex to speak individually with the people as they leave to " 'take possession of the land.' " (Joshua 1:11) In another hour or so the sanctuary is empty on one side and the parking lot empty on the other. He goes to his study and begins to look over the notes from and about persons who need visitation and counsel. The telephone rings. He looks out of the window and sees that the waters have "returned to their place and overflowed all its banks, as before." (Joshua 4:18)

In the chancel the pastor works in an atmosphere of acknowledged faith—every detail is clear, symmetrical, and purposed under the sign of redemption; in the narthex things are very different. The people, having received the benediction, now make a disorderly re-entry into a world of muddled marriages and chaotic cities, mid-life boredom and adolescent confusion, ethical ambiguity and emotional distress. The pastor who has just lifted the cup of blessing before the people now shakes hands with the man whose wife has left him for another; the pastor who has just poured the waters of baptism on the head of an infant now sees pain in the eyes of the mother whose teenager is full of angry rebellion. The pastor who has just addressed a merciful Father in prayer now arranges to visit a bitter and cynical executive who has been unexpectedly discharged from his job; the pastor who has just been confidently handling the scriptures now touches hands that are tense with anxiety and calloused in a harsh servitude.

The narthex is, of course, not sheer chaos. The signs of salvation and the continuities of blessing are evident in many—maybe most. To a visitor, perhaps, it will look like a very happy place as Christians exchange greetings and share joy. The pastor, though, picks up signs of despair in one, senses veiled pain in another, knows the adulterer's secret and the alcoholic's defeat. He knows that among these people in the days ahead there will be deaths no one expected, accidents no one thought possible, illnesses that defy diagnosis, and conflicts no one anticipated during the hour of worship. In the narthex the pastor is suddenly in a world which, though only a few steps from the chancel, is not at all quiet in adoration, not at all unanimous in trust, not at all obedient in love. Salvation is now neither unmistakably obvious nor openly acknowledged. In the chancel God's word ordered the hour of worship; in the narthex the sins of the congregation begin to write an agenda for a week of pastoral visitation and counsel, comfort and guidance. The transition is abrupt, violent, and difficult. Oral tradition has it that A. B. Davidson, the Scots scholar and preacher, said that the passage always left him feeling "mondayish." A woman met him on an Edinburgh street and gushed, "Oh, Dr. Davidson, I heard you preach yesterday and was so *uplifted!* It must be wonderful to be used by God like that." Davidson replied, "It gives me a backache."

The narthex is the place where pastoral attention begins to focus on those who fail to find their place in the covenant, who do not recognize their personal life story as congruent with the story of God's salvation. The announcement in church has usually been clear enough; it is God's will to save every person, to incorporate each created man and woman into the people of God, to graft each private history into the stock of salvation history. But many disqualify themselves, supposing that their individual experience or unique circumstances exempt them from the general truth. Guilt or willfulness or accident makes a loophole, and they assume that what is true for everyone else is not true for them. They are left out. They conclude that they are, somehow, "just not religious" and so unfit to participate in the way of faith. They form negative or neurotic identities, self-understandings unrelated to God's will and love. They feel disorganized; they experience alienation; unable to comprehend their lives as connected narratives that have meaning and make sense. The pastor knows that the story of God's revelation is a comprehensive narrative that includes everyone—how can he provide the insights and incentive to get such persons to understand their own lives as chapters, or at least paragraphs, in the epic narration of God's saving history?

Ruth and the Feast of Pentecost

Ruth is a particularly useful book for the narthex, for the story is placed in "the times the judges judged," a notoriously disordered age. In English Bibles (following the Septuagint) the book follows the chaotic era described in Judges 19—21 when "every man did what was right in his own eyes," (Judg. 21:25) and provides a quiet, out-of-the-way contrast to the wild turbulence of those decades. The more authoritative arrangement of the Hebrew Bible places Ruth among "the writings" and loses the contrast with Judges 19—21. Robert Boling, though, has recently pointed out many verbal correspondences that suggest relationships between Judges 19—21 and Ruth.[2] An original relation between Judges 19—21 and Ruth cannot be proved but it is, thanks to Boling's exegetical work, plausible. For the pastor the relation is extremely suggestive since it provides a look at what goes on between Sundays under seemingly anarchic conditions. Neither liturgists nor preachers have paid much attention to the book—no lectionary includes it in the assigned cycle of readings for public worship. There are no outstanding, historically prominent figures in Ruth, no splendid kings, no charismatic judges, no fiery prophets; it is a plain story about two widows and a farmer whose lives are woven into the fabric of God's salvation through the ordinary actions of common life.

But regardless of where it is placed in the canon, simply by being *in* the canon the story of the outsider Ruth, a person not born into the faith and who felt no natural part of it, became integrated into the larger story of God's people. Scripture is a vast tapestry of God's saving ways among his people. The great names in the plot which climaxes at Sinai (Abraham, Isaac, Joseph, Moses) and the great names in the sequel (Joshua, Samuel, David, Solomon) can be intimidating to ordinary, random individuals: "Surely there is no way that I can have any significant part in such a star-studded cast." The story of the widowed, impoverished, alien Ruth is proof to the contrary. She is the inconsequential outsider whose life is essential for telling the complete story of salvation. The concluding lines of the story have a surprise ending, "O. Henry" quality to them; "So Boaz took Ruth and she became his wife . . . and she bore a son.

. . . They named him Obed; he was the father of Jesse, the father of David." (Ruth 4:13, 17) However modest and unassuming this story is, it can never be judged insignificant—Ruth was the great-grandmother of King David! Ruth is the instance of a person uprooted, obscure, alienated who learned to understand her story as a modest but nevertheless essential part of the vast epic whose plot is designed by God's salvation.

The book of Ruth became an explicitly pastoral document when it was assigned as a reading at the Feast of Pentecost. The kerygmatic theme of Pentecost is the covenant revelation at Sinai. The Torah reading assigned to the Feast tells the story of the revelation on Mt. Sinai in Exodus 19—20 and the liturgy of the day remembers the event. At Sinai Israel found structure and direction for the redeemed life. The past was defined, the future was established, and the every-day conduct of the people was ordered within the covenant boundaries. The life of the people was not a random series of experiences, arbitrary, casual, and unpredictable. It was a *narrative*—there were plot, structure, purpose, and design. Each detail of each person's life is part of a larger story, and the larger story is salvation. At Sinai God revealed his ways and showed how all behavior and all relationships were included in the overall structure of redemption. The people found out who God was and where they stood in relation to him. In many congregations, still, (both Jewish and Christian) the first day of Pentecost is celebrated by the confirmation of young people, confirmation being an identity rite in which who we are is confirmed on the basis of what God has shown himself to be in relation to us.

The Sinai event is a kind of axle for holding together two basic realities: one, everything God does involves me (election); and two, everything I do is therefore significant (covenant). Because I am chosen, I have consequence. Election creates a unique identity; cove-nant describes a responsible relationship. Election is the declaration that God has designs upon me; covenant is the description of how the things I do fit into those designs.

The first two sentences in the Sinai revelation set the two realities side by side: " 'I am the LORD your God, who brought you out of the land of Egypt, out of the house of bondage. You shall have no other gods before me.' " (Exod. 20:2–3) The first sentence emphasizes election; the second, covenant. God's action gives significance to our lives; our lives are therefore consequential. We are consequential in two ways: we are a result (a consequence) of what God does; we are important (consequential). Because we are "persons of consequence" it makes a difference whether we do or do not have other gods, make graven images, kill, steal, etc.

Sinai, in short, is a realization that we count and what we do counts. History makes sense because God's will and humankind's will are manifest in it. Nothing is random or inconsequential or meaningless. The world of the everyday—speech, weather, topography—is overwhelmingly *actual* at Sinai. There was at Sinai an Egyptian past to make sense out of and a wilderness future to deal with, and it was all done in the company of other persons who had grumbled their way out of Egypt, each of whom had a name and a genealogy. Sinai was not a special, holy place to which the people had come on pilgrimage. It was where they happened to be when God's will was clarified and the people's response was recognized. Decisions were made there, and it was, therefore, a decisive event.

George Ernest Wright expands on how this immersion in history uniquely shaped Israel's faith:

> The sense of the goodness and meaningfulness of life and of the true nature of personality were achieved in a context of communion, interdependence and relatedness. The worth of man was seen, not so much as a natural possession or right, as it was a right conferred by or derived from God. Personality achieved its true depth and stature in a relation of faith, love and unqualified obedience to God. God has set his love on man and man was to respond in gratitude with a sense of imperative obligation. The problem of life was analysed, therefore, not over against nature and the question of security within it, but in the much deeper relation with the will of God who created nature and called society into being. Primary attention was accordingly focused on the problem of the will. The will of man in relation to the will of God was the central problem of existence.[3]

From that time on, when Israel wrote about God, she wrote history. Among other peoples in the ancient world there was nothing comparable. Israel's neighbors wrote down historical data—the reign of kings, lists of cities conquered in battle, treaty obligations, business transactions—but none of them wrote *history,* narratives in which the decisions of people and the response they lived were told in relation to the decisions of God and his actions. When Israel's contemporaries wrote about God, they wrote myths and legends—hearsay gossip about the gods, not true stories about persons.

The Hebrews were the world's first historians. Because they were convinced that God worked among them where they were, each day, they believed that what they did, whether in faith or unbelief, sin or righteousness, obedience or rebellion, was significant. Because it was significant, it was capable of being narrated as a story, that is, as an account in which what people did had consequences and was part of a structured purpose. A story begins, has a middle, and ends. Everything in it has a point, a meaning. Nothing is irrelevant. Each character, however minor, plays a part. And so the Hebrews wrote *history* of men and women created in the image of God, while their contemporaries wrote myths of the gods, imagined in the image of their neighbors.

This historical consciousness meant that existence was not imposed on a person from without, nor was it inherent in things as they were—it was a gift, offered to God's people in a developed interplay of wills. Acceptance would mean one thing, rejection another. The way the story developed was not fixed. What was certain was that there was a story: God's will and man's will both had meaning, the meanings interacted and provided the content for the narration. Because the Hebrews had this lively sense of *story,* they did not look upon the covenant, which was, in a sense, the syntax of the story, as a legal burden to be borne; it was evidence, rather, of the significance and interrelated meanings of every detail in history. The Hebrews would no more have considered the covenant ten commandments as a burden in living a life of faith than a person would call nouns, verbs, and prepositions a burden in carrying on a conversation.

This historical consciousness of Israel, made from the stuff of election and covenant, has been thoroughly discussed by biblical scholars and does not need further elaboration here.[4] It is enough simply to emphasize that it was at this *kind* of feast, a feast in which worship was immersed in history, that Ruth was read, for the pastoral uses of Ruth are dependent on this context. The use of Ruth as a reading at Pentecost adds nothing, as such, to the historically rooted Sinai revelation. What it does is to provide an application of this theologically conceived history among persons who are out of the mainstream of the story, who did not have an ancestor at Sinai, and who could easily have been left out or otherwise overlooked. Since it is precisely this kind of person to whom a great deal of pastoral work is directed, the book of Ruth, in this setting, provides extensive help in doing it.

The Short Story

For pastoral work, the most important implication of the book of Ruth is simply its form: it is a story. Form critics have attempted to trace its development and demonstrate its provenance in the field of ancient literature, but they have not been successful. It is, as E. F. Campbell, Jr., has shown, "a new form."[5] There is nothing quite like it in ancient literature.

A people who learned to understand their lives historically, that is, as a connected, meaningful existence in which God's will mixed with their free will in ways which demonstrated purpose, created the story form in order to show instances of this purposed, coherent history in local, daily situations among ordinary people. The striking thing about Ruth, especially as it is read in the context of the Pentecost worship, is the way ". . . it brings the lofty concept of covenant into vital contact with day-to-day life, not at the royal court or in the temple, but right here in the narrow compass of village life."[6] The Hebrew short story was never a simple entertainment, an Arabian Nights diversion, but always an exploration of a particular way in which the interaction of personal wills (God's will, my will, my neighbor's will) took shape in the "everyday doings of random persons."[7]

The comprehensive kerygmatic narratives were shaped by Israel's theological historians, the so-called Yahwist, Elohist, Deuteronomist, and Priestly writers. The short story was created by someone who was immersed in the Sinai covenant traditions and felt the need to provide a similarly compelling account of God's ways in terms of a few ordinary people within limited circumstances.

For the pastor this is important for it means that we have a model for taking seriously each person, however obscure, however unimportant, however "out of it." There are many people who do not recognize that they have anything in common with what they hear in the church's preaching and teaching, or find any parallels between their inner life and what is expressed in the worship of the community of faith. Worse, they sometimes, by selective observation and listening, feel deliberately excluded, like Naomi who was sure that God had pronounced "evil sentence on me." (1:21, author's translation) Ruth, hearing only the narratives of the Penteteuch, as a Moabitess could only have concluded that she was left out of God's designs. Persons who are obscure and unnoticed, or who have drifted and become embittered, or who have experienced systematic rejection in the society, listen to the larger story but fail to find their place in it—they don't see where they fit. The short story, by beginning where they are and concentrating on the problem of their life-situation (the complaints of a Naomi, the alienation of a Ruth) is able to shape the details of their particular suffering or despair or emptiness into a connected, ordered story that can be, then, seen as an aspect of the larger narration. "All things are more bearable," says Joseph Sittler, "if we make a story of them. And ultimate desolations are made both more bearable and significant when the story is the Ultimate Story."[8]

The short story is a pastoral tool for moving from the kerygmatic center of Israel's theologians to the outlying peripheral people who feel left out of salvation history. In the process of telling the story of their lives (or better, teaching them to tell it), their names and struggles, their sins and disappointments are rearranged into a plot that has a beginning in God, a providential middle, and a conclusion in salvation. No biblical story is *just* a story, any more so than any person's story—each deals with actual events and traditions in which there is a Creator, Director, and Redeemer, with whom ordinary persons in history get involved.[9]

The short story is the pastoral form for narrating *heilsgeschichte* (salvation history) in the vocabulary of *seelsgeschichte* (soul history). In the *heilsgeschichte* of Judges, for instance, the enmity of the Midianites is kerygmatically integrated into the historical narrative and shown to be a part of salvation; in the *seelsgeschichte* of Ruth the bitter empti-

ness of Naomi is pastorally attended to under the dynamics of providence and guided to a concluding fullness. In the *heilsgeschicte* of
Exodus the formidable and unyielding Egyptians are judged and
defeated in the catastrophic plagues and miraculous sea crossing; in
the *seelsgeschicte* of Ruth the everyday ordinariness of gleaning in the
barley fields is used as a means for accomplishing redemption. In the
heilsgeschicte of Joshua the gigantically-walled fortress city Jericho is
surrounded and conquered by the total community of God in colorful parade, accompanied by brilliantly sounding trumpets, and the
promised land is entered; in the *seelsgeschicte* of Ruth an old levirate
law is patiently and quietly worked through by some old men at the
city gates of provincial Bethlehem, and a link is forged in the genealogical chain of the Messiah.

By taking a storyteller's approach to the outsider, pastoral work
is saved from two egregious (but, unfortunately, common) errors,
namely, moralism and condescension. Pastoral moralism focuses on
what is wrong with the misfit and, by concentrating on the trouble,
alienates him or her even further. Moralistic hectoring is a parody
of moral relationships. The person who doesn't feel at home in the
assembly of God's people has, of course, very often done something
wrong; but to bypass all the complexities of the life-situation and
apply a moral to the symptom only compounds the difficulty. The
pastors are historians not moralists. They learn their craft at the feet
of the great theological historians of Sinai, and from their direct
descendants, the four Gospel writers, not by collecting aphorisms in
the fields of the Roman Stoics. If pastors only carry moral sayings in
their pockets and go through the parish sticking them, like gummed
labels, on the victims of the week, there will be no good pastoral
work; they must learn how to be gospel storytellers. After the manner of the storyteller of Ruth, they must become skilled in making
a story out of the details of a particular trouble, using the plot design
and vocabulary that they have assimilated from, say, the Deuteronomist. The storytelling pastor differs from the moralizing pastor in the
same way that a responsible physician differs from a clerk in a drugstore. When an ill person goes to a physician, the physician "takes
a history" before offering a diagnosis and writing a prescription. The
presumption is that everything that a person has experienced is

relevant to the illness and must be taken into account if there is to be a healing. The clerk in the drugstore simply sells a patent medicine off the shelf—one thing for headaches, another for heartburn, another for indigestion—without regard for the particular details of a person's pain. Biblical pastoral work "takes a history" and with that raw material creates a story of salvation, like the Ruth story fashioned out of famine, widowhood, barley harvest, levirite law, God's steadfast love, providence and peace, the town of Bethlehem, and the land of Moab. The storyteller assembles the local, personal, and seemingly disparate details along with the numerous individual items that were never mentioned in the histories developed out of Sinai, and makes a history that is significant, meaningful, and redemptive.

Condescension is the other pastoral error to which storytelling is a prevention. Pastors are very frequently bored with dull people, irritated with difficult people, and frustrated by incalcitrant people. Persons who don't sing the hymns heartily, who don't tithe faithfully, who don't attend worship regularly, who don't read the Bible intelligently, who don't love maturely—all these persons are the bane of pastoral life. It is not surprising that the pastor—who does sing the hymns robustly, tithe generously, is always at worship, who brings a well-trained mind to the reading of the Bible, and whom, it goes without saying, is mature in his love—should find it hard not to be condescending towards many if not most of his parishioners. But if these same persons are approached with the interests and expectations of a storyteller everything changes.If each parishioner is a key person in a story, everything is alive and interesting. All the details of the day are relevant. A storyteller is unwilling to reduce anyone to the formula of a case history, or depersonalize anyone into a statistic in the divorce rate, or use someone as an illustration of menopause depression. Stories enhance, elaborate, and develop. Each detail, by being arranged in its proper place, is perceived to make a difference. Existence is not flattened out on the graph paper of analysis; it comes alive in the movements of a drama in which some of the actions and speeches are still to be written. Chesterton says ". . . a story is exciting because it has in it so strong an element of will, of what theology calls free-will. You cannot finish a sum how you like. But you can finish a story how you like."[10]

Pastoral work that is rooted in the covenant histories that derive from Sinai and develops the storytelling skills that are represented in Ruth is safe from both moralistic practices and condescending attitudes. It continues the healthy, person-respecting, purpose-evoking ministry which is inherent in the way of Israel. For Israel, when she wanted to speak of her faith, did not do it in moralistic terms, or through sociological surveys, or in conceptual essays—there were neither philosophers nor statisticians nor belletrists in Israel: "people simply told a story."[11]

For persons who are familiar with the way Sinai's historians created a narrative, talking is not the first step in pastoral storytelling. Listening is the first step. It is the precondition for creating the pastoral short story, that is, making the transition from what a person perceives as alienation and experiences as a jumble of unrelated irrelevancies to a sense of coherence and belonging. When a pastor listens to a parishioner with patient intensity, the very act of listening gives narrative sense to what would otherwise be only trivial gossip, or a fragment of complaint, or an isolated anecdote. The sustained attentive listening imparts meaning to what a person says: details can be perceived to have significance if a person listens to them significantly. But without someone who is willing to take an interest in the mixed, random material of everyday life, the patience to ponder it, the skill to discern the thread of meaning in it, and the wisdom to fill in the lacunae with frequently omitted but obvious items of reality like the providence of God, the person's story will not get told. But by taking everyday things in a serious vein, an inner structure is realized in them—random persons and events are embedded in the structures of salvation history. The pastoral act of listening enables a person to recognize correspondences between what is denigrated and devaluated by others as mundane with the actual patterns of God's redemption. There is a remarkable instance of this recognized correspondence in the story of Ruth when the storyteller works out a connection between the way God acts and the way the people in the story act. Boaz introduces Ruth to the " 'God of Israel, under whose wings you have come to take refuge!' " Later, at the threshing floor, Ruth asks Boaz to "spread therefore thy skirt over thine handmaid." (2:12 and 3:9, K.J.V.) "Wings" and "skirt" are the same word in Hebrew, forcing a recognition that what Boaz promises Ruth that God will do for her is worked out in what Ruth gets Boaz to do for her: the providence of God appears under the forms of ordinary personal encounter.

The pastor begins this work then, not so much as a storyteller, but as one who believes that there is a story to be told, the curiosity to be attentive to the life of another, and the determination to listen through the apparently rambling digressions until a plot begins to emerge. He is a regional worker, a plodder who prefers to pry open the vents of one stuffy, closed-up life, than to dazzle, with melodramatics, a crowd of diversion hungry dilettantes. Such pastoral attention is heuristic, discovering in every fresh encounter with the commonplace a new aspect of the story. The nineteenth-century French clinician Laënnec used to say to his students: "Listen, listen to your patient! He is giving you the diagnosis." Laënnec was a good physician; he invented the stethoscope.

Counseling and Visitation

The pastoral act of listening, which is the pastor's major contribution in the creation of stories, takes place ordinarily during arranged acts of counseling and visitation. Since storymaking and storytelling require a certain degree of leisure and privacy—time to pay attention and a place free from interruption—they will not take place unless care is taken to make the necessary arrangements. Storytelling must not take place in the chancel, for no one wants his or her story extemporized from the pulpit, and it cannot take place in the narthex for there is too much distraction and too little time. But both visitation and counseling provide the conditions in which a short story of salvation can be constructed out of the everyday materials that come to light in such conversations.

I distinguish between counseling and visitation only in terms of their external arrangements. Counseling is usually initiated by a person asking for help and takes place in the pastor's study at his or her convenience; visitation is usually initiated by the pastor and takes place in a parishioner's home at his or her convenience. In counseling, the pastor ordinarily has more control; in visitation, the parishioner has more control. In my study I can exclude interruptions and define the relationship, but when I am in someone's living room, I am not free to turn off the television, take the telephone off the hook, or tell the vacuum cleaner salesperson to come back another day. This, of course, is why many pastors prefer counseling over visitation—they are recognized as an expert by someone who admits a need, they are clearly in charge, and they are able to arrange the terms of the relationship to suit themselves. It also accounts for the fact that most church members value visitation more highly, for in that pastoral act they are singled out for special attention and recognized as important; and they can regulate the level of intimacy in the conversation to suit themselves: if they are so inclined, they can bare their hearts; or if they wish, they can keep the conversation superficial and anecdotal. But when the pastor actively sets out to collaborate with people in the creative work of storymaking, using the structures of counseling and visitation to do it, the traditional stereotypes of the two pastoral acts escape these ego-distinctions (who is most important? who is in control?) and become, simply, complementary ways of doing the same thing, viz., getting at the story. Neither is then preferred over the other, for the difference is not in what takes place but only in the setting. In either case, all that is needed, is an arrangement in which everyday conversation can be treated confidentially and purposefully, so that a sense of collaboration can be established, so much as to say, "We are going to talk together, and we are going to make a *story* out of our conversation. We are going to find where we, together, fit in the plot of God's story." In such an arrangement the pastor does not *tell* the story, he or she merely affirms the fact that there is a story to be told, and goes on to provide the opportunity and stimulus for persons to construct and tell their own stories as personal and local instances of the story of covenant salvation.

When approached this way, weekday counseling and visitation are to the Sunday preaching what the story of Ruth is to the Feast of Pentecost, that is, what the short story is to the theological history. The storymaking metaphor restores both counseling and visitation to a biblical setting, from which they have been dislodged in an age of secularization. For the fact is that both the popularity of counseling and the unpopularity of visitation are in considerable part due to their secularization, having been torn out of their biblical milieu and pursued as activities with their own justification. Counseling has become secularized under the influence of the psychological sciences and visitation under the influence of the public relations industry. By learning how to use them as a means for storytelling and storymaking, they can easily be restored to their original settings and do good service as biblically informed pastoral work.

As a counselor, the pastor is secularized away from being a friend in Christ into functioning as a substitute for God, which is, in effect, an act of idolatry. It is an extremely difficult process to resist, for who does not like to be treated as a god? The person who comes for counseling has the expectation that he or she, the weak one, will be helped by the strong pastor. The inferior comes to the superior. Persons look for experts to solve their problems for them so that they will not have to acquire competence to live authentically and responsibly. They are used to deferring to experts in every other area of life, why not here?

Jesus provided a masterful refutation of this particular kind of secularization in his response to the enthusiastic sycophancy of the man who ran up, knelt before him, and said, " 'Good Teacher, what must I do to inherit eternal life?' " Jesus rejected the idolatrous position in which the greeting placed him and said, " 'Why do you call me good? No one is good but God alone.' " (Mark 10:17–18) While the man's address might be justified on later christological grounds, under the circumstances it can only be seen as an attempt to put Jesus in the role of responsible expert and himself in the role of helpless amateur. As a person practiced in the ways of buying and selling for a profit, he knew how to put himself in an inferior position in order to get what he needed: turn Jesus into a counselor, from whom he could buy advice on eternal life. Jesus refused the role and insisted that both of them were on the same level—" 'You know the commandments,' " that is, we both have access to the same revelation. The man's response showed, despite his initial dishonesty in approaching Jesus, an honest desire for goodness, and Jesus loved him for it. Jesus' love is to be distinguished from a condescending pity or an alienating criticism. His love made them peers and provided for the conditions of creative collaboration. Jesus then spotted an empty place in the man's life and gave the command that would fill in the missing material with which, together, they could make a story out of what had, up to that time, been only compulsive listmaking: so many commandments kept, so many possessions acquired. All the man had to do was to join Jesus in incorporating the new data into his life. He chose to reject the offer. Good counseling does not aim to be "successful," and has no control over how the newly introduced or uncovered reality will be used. The pastor cannot "write" the story alone—only collaborate with the other in the writing, and the telling, of it.

The pastor participates in the making of a story, not in an adjustment; the primary interest is in getting at usable truth, and then taking the person seriously as an equal so that there is confidence and freedom to be creative with the material. By resisting "secularization," that is, refusing to be used apart from or in place of God, the pastor forces the person to deal with God on his or her own. The purpose of the pastor is to assist in assembling all the relevant reality, which includes God, and then to encourage the telling of the story coherently. The pastor must not twist everything into a happy ending or simplify it into a homily. Some of the stories will be happy, some sad, some comic, some tragic, but all of them will be true.

The secularization of pastoral visitation takes place when the pastor gives up the uncertain and somewhat modest work of being a companion to persons in pilgrimage and takes on the job of public relations agent for the congregation; the job then is to whip up flagging enthusiasm, raise money for the budget, promote new programs, and "get out the vote" on Sundays. Even when people sense the manipulative nature of such visitation, they don't seem to mind —they are so conditioned to being treated in such ways by advertisers, politicians, and salespeople, they apparently assume that it is the mark of any successful person and admire the energy of the pastor who does it.

When such visitation goes well, there are substantial rewards; when it goes badly, the pastor is fired and another hired. In any given instance the announced purpose of the visitation is religious and so disguises the secularization of the means. But the plain fact is that under the pressure of such expectations, visitation ceases to be pastoral work. Pastors who sense the secularization of such visitation rightly refuse to do it. Martin Thornton writes, "Visiting people in their homes may be inspired by . . . blunt recruitment, which I must oppose; 'a visiting parson makes a churchgoing people' is either luckily false or regrettably true."[12]

The pastor's task is to maintain the integrity of visitation, even when the practice of other pastors and the expectation of parishioners has diverged from biblical ministry. St. Paul did pastoral visitation in cities that were inundated with sophists—itinerant religious professionals, who visited towns, villages, and market places promoting religious programs for a fee. The parallel to pastoral visitation is not exact, for the pastor is a resident, and the sophist was an itinerant, but there are resemblances in that in both cases there is a "going to" the people where they are with an expectation that the layperson will "get something out of it." Paul strenuously dissociated himself from the kind of visitation practiced by the sophists. One thing that Paul did in reclaiming visitation as a tool for story-making was to make it very clear that the visitation was not "professional"—he had not been hired to do the public and difficult parts of religion for the people: "Not that we lord it over your faith; *we work with you* for your joy." (2 Cor. 1:24, author's emphasis) Neither does he have anything to sell them: "For we are not, like so many, peddlers of God's word; but as men of sincerity, as commissioned by God, in the sight of God we speak in Christ." (2 Cor. 2:17) He insists that in his visitation he is simply participating in a common vocation of discipleship with them; there is nothing exalted about his position, he is not over them, or beyond them: "We have this treasure in earthen vessels." (2 Cor. 4:7) Paul's fondness for prefixing the words for Christian vocation with *syn* is further evidence of this. In the AV it is translated fellow (fellow citizen, fellow heir, fellow helper, fellow laborer, fellow prisoner, fellow servant, fellow soldier, fellow worker, etc.). Whatever Paul is, and whatever people are—they are in it together, they are *com*panions in faith. The pastoral visit is not the condescending visit of the superior to the inferior, and not the professional visit of one who has something to one who does not have it. It is an act of collaboration in order to demonstrate the mutuality of the Christian discipleship. Paul's inventiveness in finding ways to express this comes through vividly in a sentence in his letter to the Ephesians where he uses three *syn-* compounds in succession. He describes the Gentiles as "fellow heirs *[sugkleronoma,]* members of the same body *[sussoma,]* and partakers of *[summetrocha]* the promise in Christ Jesus through the gospel." (Eph. 3:6)

The second thing that Paul did to re-establish the visit as an authentic pastoral act was to use the visit to share his own experience in Christ. 2 Corinthians, the most autobiographical of all Paul's writings, is the best example of this. Paul uses the letter to share his troubles, his despair, his hurt. His willingness to expose himself as a weak and troubled co-Christian, makes the Corinthians participants with him in the life of faith. A contemporary instance of such personal sharing is given by the psychotherapist, Sheldon Kepp, who decided to share with his patients the hellish journey through brain surgery and the inadequacies and failures that showed up in his responses:

> Some people both wanted and did not want to hear the upsetting parts. But most agreed that my sharing made me seem more human to them. In fact, by revealing so much of my own still unresolved feelings and problems, I made some patients feel freer and more hopeful about themselves. If I were still so imperfect, perhaps they did not have so far to go.[13]

That is exactly the impact that the great confessional passages, 2 Corinthians 4:7–18 ("we have this treasure in earthen vessels . . ."), 6:1–13 ("We are treated as imposters . . ."), 11:16–30 ("I will boast of the things that show my weakness . . ."), would have on Paul's fellow pilgrims, for he makes it clear that his proposed visit is not something that is done for them or to them. It is a demonstration of common faith, an exercise in collegiality in the ordinary work of following Christ. When visitation is an instance of collaboration and companionship, it can be used for storymaking. The pastor is God's spy searching out ways of grace. Combining what he or she finds, along with what the other has found, together they can write a story. The pastor listens, helps arrange the data, calls attention to unnoticed material, suggests the rearrangement of a sentence here, the change of a preposition there. The effect of Paul's work was to wrest the visit from the hands of the sophist peddlers and propagandists and to establish control over it so that it could be used effectively for developing local and individual participation in the life of Christ (what I am calling "making your own story"). Paul's reclamation work has to be done over and over again if visitation is to be for the pastor and not the pastor for visitation.

In some ways both counseling and visitation are minimal pastoral acts: the pastor doesn't *do* very much. God is at work before we come on the scene and continues to work after we leave it. The pastor doesn't introduce God into anyone's life. (God was "long beforehand with my soul.")[14] The pastor simply calls attention to what is already there, and by skilled listening on the one hand and a stubborn resistance to being "secularized" on the other provides the conditions in which a gospel story can be told. We encourage the use of material which has been suppressed (sin, for instance, which is hard to acknowledge, or failures which are hard to admit); we stimulate the recognition of grace which up to that point had not been consciously perceived. The pastor, by assuming that God has designs upon this person (election) and that God has provided a structure in which salvation can be experienced (covenant), bridges the distance from Sinai to wherever the person happens to be at that moment and offers the conviction that there is a good story of providence, or salvation, or sanctification to be told.

Not every act of visitation and counsel will produce a finished story. By no means! But all pastoral counsel and visitation can be an aspect of storymaking. The pastor provides in his or her vocation the confidence that the materials for a story are there. Pastoral counsel and visitation protect and affirm the singularity of the ordinary individual so that the uniqueness and meaning of life are not lost in the thunder and lightning of the great story that is proclaimed at Sinai. Such pastoral work substantiates Charles Williams' observation that in Christendom ". . . her spectacles and her geniuses are marvellous, but her unknown saints are her power."[15]

Many will choose not to participate in such work: neither counseling nor visitation, even if done well, guarantee that a story will be created. All pastors can do in counsel and visitation is courteously invite persons to make and tell stories, and offer themselves as skilled collaborators in the work. If the person does not want to engage in the work, there is nothing the pastor can do about that. What we must not do is impatiently and hurriedly throw a story together on our own—it won't be real and the person will know it. It will be propaganda to promote a cause or a half-truth anecdote to illustrate a doctrine, but it won't be a story.

Naomi, Ruth, and Boaz

The book of Ruth, as a single instance of local storymaking in the context of the great salvation story of Israel and Church, is only a sample of what is possible. It is evidence that it can be done and provides stimulus for others to do it. But every person has to find his or her own way into the story. The church is not a casting room to which people come to try out for a limited number of roles, and then, if selected, live them out under the direction of the pastor, and if rejected, go off to live an ordinary life as best they can on their own. The pastoral task is not to assign roles or direct roles but to help persons "get into the story," just as they are, doing the things that are appropriate for each, and responding to the others who are in it with them. The three main characters in Ruth—Naomi, Ruth, and Boaz—show three ways of getting into the story. Each shows, from quite different beginnings and in quite different ways, the steady emergence and growth of individual meaning through inner urgencies, the development of what is individual out of what is typical within the spacious arena of salvation history where there is ample room for creative diversities. None of these ways, nor any others, must be used to impose a biblical role on another.

Naomi got into the story by complaining. She experienced loss, complained bitterly about it, had her unhappiness taken seriously by the storyteller and formulated into a complaint against God. No material could have seemed less promising as the raw data for a gospel story than that which is provided in the first chapter of Ruth: a famine, three deaths, three widows, and anarchy.

When Naomi returned home to Bethlehem after her ten-year absence, there was excitement and a readiness to rejoice at her homecoming, but Naomi refused the welcome.

"Don't call me 'Sweet One,'
Call me 'Bitter One,'
For Shadday has made me bitter indeed.
I was full when I went away,
But empty Yahweh has brought me back.
Why call me 'Sweet One'?
For Yahweh has testified against me
And Shadday has pronounced evil sentence on me."
                    (1:20–21)[16]

This is worded in such a way that Naomi is presented as a complainant before God. This style of complaint, put into legal form, is also represented by Jeremiah who engaged in suit and countersuit between God and the people, and pressed a legal case against God in the face of the evidence that God had failed to be just and fair.

Though it seems impious, and even blasphemous to some, the plain fact is that such formalized complaints are fairly common in scripture. The pastor can help a person "get into the story" by assisting in the formulation of complaints, making out lists of grievances, clarifying where God has failed to do his part, and drawing up an indictment against him. The pastor doesn't always have to be on God's side, defending him; there are times when the biblical position is at the plaintiff's side. There are instances when pastors encourage complaint, knowing that

> . . . not only is complaint tolerated by God, but it can even be the proper stance of a person who takes God seriously! Anyone who ascribes full sovereignty to a just and merciful God may expect to encounter the problem of theodicy, and to wrestle with that problem is no sin, even when it leads to an attempt to put God on trial. Petulant Jonah, earnest Jeremiah, persistent Job—Naomi stands in the company.[17]

By being taken seriously—not rejected, not toned down, not spiritualized—Naomi's complaint becomes part of the story. The emptiness of her life is woven into the plot, and in the process is the occasion for demonstrating God's providence. Her emptiness encounters a symbolic filling when Ruth returns from the threshing floor with a generous gift of barley from Boaz; " 'You shall not go empty to your mother-in-law.' " (3:17)[18] She who had returned empty to Bethlehem was empty no longer. Providence was on the move! The emptiness is reversed finally at the conclusion of the story when the village women shout, after the birth of Obed, "A son is born to Naomi!" Not "to Ruth" but "to Naomi." By having her complaint taken into the story Naomi does not get an explanation of God's ways, rather she finds herself in a living, developing set of relationships which extend into the future. In sometimes slight, and occasionally dramatic, ways she realizes that the faithful God, in spite of all appearances, is still about his business, and that frees her to go about hers.

If her complaint (if anyone's) had been edited out of the story —rejected as a vagrant whine, judged unsuitable for inclusion in a story about salvation—it would have festered and become virulent criticism of everyone except God. By getting into the story it became a means for experiencing the ways of God's providence.

Ruth got into the story by asking for what she wanted. At one point, approaching the dramatic climax in the story, Ruth was coached by her mother-in-law in how to approach Boaz. They were both aware that Boaz had a kinsman-redeemer relationship to them, and knew that if their cards were played right they both could be rescued from poverty and that Ruth could get a husband. The threshing floor was assigned as the place of their meeting. Naomi coached Ruth,

> "Now is it not so that Boaz is one of our covenant circle, with whose girls you have been? Notice, he is winnowing (the grain of) the threshing floor near the gate this very night. Now bathe and anoint yourself, don your cape, and go down to the threshing floor. Do not make yourself known to the man until he has finished eating and drinking. And when he lies down, note the place where he lies, and go and uncover his legs and lie down. Then he will tell you what you are to do." (3:2–4)[19]

The interesting thing in this part of the story is that Ruth does exactly what her mother-in-law tells her to do—except for the last item. For when we next see Ruth at the threshing floor later that night, lying beside Boaz, the narration continues:

> Around midnight, the man shuddered and groped about; and here was a woman lying next to him! He said, "Who are you?" and she said, "I am Ruth your maid-servant. Now spread your 'wing' over your maid-servant, for you are a redeemer." (3:8–9)[20]

Naomi had told Ruth ". . . he will tell you what you are to do," but when the time came, Ruth took the initiative and told Boaz what she wanted him to do, ". . . spread your 'wing' over your maidservant, for you are a redeemer." There is a wordplay here between Yahweh's wings in 2:12 and the "wings" or "corners" of Boaz' garment. "Commentators frequently invoke ancient and modern Arabic custom as further evidence that the placing of a garment over a woman is a symbolic claim to marriage."[21] In other words, Ruth said, "I want you to marry me." The exact correspondence of terminology between Ezekiel 16:8 and Ruth 3:9 is strong evidence that Ruth's request of Boaz is marriage.

This sudden intrusion of freewill, Ruth assertively taking the initiative, would hardly be lost on any who are paying attention to the story. Ruth is not a victim. Being in God's story does not mean passively letting things happen to us. It does not mean dumb submission, nor blind obedience. Alien though she is (and her foreignness is repeatedly emphasized; six times she is called "the Moabitess") and outside the defined covenant boundaries, she gets into the story when she steps out of the social roles in which she has been placed by others—the roles of daughter-in-law, Moabitess, gleaner—and speaks her own lines. The consequence is that she enters into the center action and becomes an ancester of the Messiah.

There are times when the pastor collaborates in storymaking by encouraging persons to step out and speak their own lines—not just parrot that in which they have been coached by mother and father, spouse and teachers, or even the pastor. Storymaking is creative not only in its arranging of materials, not only in paying attention to the overlooked realities of the hidden ways of God, but, at the right time, speaking up on one's own and asking for what we want.

Boaz got into the story by taking up new responsibilities. Before anything else he was represented in the story as a person of good reputation and solid prosperity. He was on good terms with the people in his fields. Everyone seemed pleased to have him around. He was described as a "man of substance." (2:1)[22] His name means "in him is strength."[23]

We know that the story was set in a time in history when "every [person] did what was right in his [or her] own eyes." It was every person for him or herself, and the devil take the hindmost. During a time when "might is right" are all people of strength bullies? Do people of substance only take care of themselves at the expense of the widows and the poor? A background theme of Ruth has to do with covenant responsibilities as they are expressed in "redeemer" obligations and levirate marriage. The exact responsibilities involved in these ancient legal codes and customs are not clear; what is clear is that there were obligations, and part of the interest of the story hangs on whether Boaz will or will not meet them. Boaz could have dodged his responsibilities, apparently, and still kept his good name since there was another in a more responsible position than he was. He could have kept the letter of the law by referring the matter of Ruth to the nearer kinsman, "Mr. So-and-So."

The scene at the city gate in which the redeemer obligations are worked out makes it clear that Boaz, the "man of substance," will live up to his name.

> Then Boaz said to the elders and to all the people, "You are witnesses today, that I hereby buy all that belonged to Elimelek and all that belonged to Kilyon and Mahlon from the hand of Naomi. And, more important, Ruth the Moabitess, wife of Mahlon, I 'buy' as my wife,
>
> To establish the name of the dead on his inheritance,
>   So that the name of the dead not be cut off
>   From among his brethren
>   Or from the assembly of his town.
> You are witnesses—today!" (4:9–10)[24]

Some people, like Boaz, get into the story by taking up their responsibilities. The plunge into righteous living, which models God's righteous relationships by going beyond the letter of the law and persistently and generously seeking for ways to put their wealth and position to work on behalf of others. Because Boaz decided to act in this way, God's "wings" are experienced in the story through the "wings" of Boaz (2:13 and 3:9). Redemption is experienced in the story, because Boaz works through the legal details of an old Mosaic law. There are persons of "substance" who take their strength, their wealth, and their influence for granted and never use it in relation to others. Pastors are in a position to collaborate in the making of these persons' stories in such a way that they no longer see themselves as a center to which fame, possessions, and power naturally gravitate, but at the center of a circle of responsibilities. Boaz is named in the story as " 'one of our circle of redeemers.' " (2:20)[25] He knew that the function of the redeemer was

> to function on behalf of persons and their property within the circle of the larger family; . . . to take responsibility for the unfortunate and stand as their supporters and advocates. . . . to embody the basic principle of caring responsibility for those who may not have justice done for them by the unscrupulous, or even by the person who lives by the letter of the law.[26]

The story gave him the opportunity to live up to the privilege of his responsibilities, and he seized it.

There is a great deal more in this deceptively simple tale. The story is marvelously complex, full of subtle interrelationships and carefully articulated emphases. In addition to the aggressively complaining Naomi, meekly valorous Ruth, and trustworthy, responsible Boaz, there are the anonymous chorus of village women, the unnamed young man who was overseer of the harvesters, Orpah in chapter one, and the nearer kinsman in chapter four, who lived up to their obligations but no more. They also "get into the story." For anyone, in fact, can get into it. The pastor because of the thoroughness with which he or she understands the comprehensive story of God's redemption is often in a key position to assist persons to begin, just as they are and just where they are, to tell stories that turn out every bit as good as Ruth. Repeated readings of Ruth, in the context of the grand sweep of theological history, will show up nuances and release insights that suggest numerous ways in which pastoral work can join persons in talking about their lives in such a way that they will find themselves part of the story.

The Genealogy

Ruth is important for pastors insofar as it makes a quiet, private place away from the crashing kerygmatic thunder of Pentecost worship, where some ordinary people can learn to tell their own stories of love and salvation, of providence and blessing. It is an instance of pastoral work that finds a protected place and time, apart from the mountain vistas and offers to a few at a time the attention and interest that will encourage them to examine the everyday, apparently random data of their unremarkable lives, and discover the presence of grace and the storyline of redemption. It was said of the Hasid, Levi-Yitzhak of Berditchev, that "The destitute, the ignorant, the misfits sought him out. His presence made them feel important; he gave them what they needed most: dignity."[27] But having done that, the pastor must also lead them back to the mountain where, with the company of the redeemed, they will be able to share the wider joy and learn the larger mission of God's people. Having "strengthened the stakes" it is also necessary to "lengthen the cords." (Isa. 54:2)

The concluding words of Ruth at first reading seem banal: ". . . they gave him the name Obed; he was the father of Jesse, father of David." (4:17)[28] At a later time an appendix was added:

> Now this is the line of Perez: Perez begot Hezron; and Hezron begot Ram; and Ram begot Amminadab; and Amminadab begot Nahshon; and Nahshon begot Salma; and Salma begot Boaz; and Boaz begot Obed; and Obed begot Jesse; and Jesse begot David. (4:18–22)[29]

But what at first appears as an inappropriately lifeless conclusion to this very lively story, on reflection quickens the pulse. What it does, in the most succinct and laconic style, is insert this marvelously intimate realization of personalized salvation into the greater picture of God's ways. Ruth is a story in its own right, but it is not a gospel story if it is read in isolation. It is a single, luminous detail in the epic narration of cosmic salvation. The genealogy is the literary device to make a transition from a microscopic examination of how God works in an out-of-the-way place among out-of-the-way people to a telescopic vision of the immense reaches of God's ways. It does it without calling attention to itself and without in the least detracting from the intensity, the importance, or the wholeness of the story. It merely says, "Now it is time to return to the public worship of Pentecost, where we hear and celebrate all that God has done, what he will do, and what he is doing in all other places with all other peoples." Lovely as Emily Dickenson's preference is for keeping the Sabbath by "staying at home, with a bobolink for a chorister and orchard for a throne,"[30] if indulged, results in a spiritual condition of narrow smugness and cloying sentimentality.

Ruth's genealogical appendix is thus highly functional, unlike its veriform namesake which is so routinely excised from our bodies. The storyteller who attached it was thoroughly sensitive to the impact that it would have.

The genealogical lists in the Bible, synonymous in so many minds with tedium, are, in fact, documentation for the most exciting parts of the story. For the gospel does not address a faceless, nameless mob, but persons. The history of salvation is thick with names. The name is the form of speech by which a person is singled out for personal love, particular intimacy, and exact responsibilities. The biblical fondness for genealogical lists is not pedantic antiquarianism, it is a search for personal involvement, a quest for a sense of personal place in the web of relationships in which God fashions salvation.

That great storyteller, George MacDonald, knew how important the name was. In his exposition of Revelation 2:17 ("To him who conquers . . . I will give him a white stone, with a new name written on the stone which no one knows except him who receives it") he wrote:

> "The giving of the White Stone with the new name is the communication of what God thinks about the man to the man. . . . The true name is one which expresses the character, the nature, the meaning of the person who bears it. . . . Who can give a man this, his own name? God alone. For no one but God sees what the man is. . . . It is only when the man has become his name that God gives him the stone with his name upon it, for then first can he understand what his name signifies."[31]

Matthew 1, which provides the genealogy of Jesus, is familiar with Ruth 4. Matthew's genealogy is highly unconventional in that it interrupts the traditional male listing by inserting four women: Tamar, Rahab, Ruth, and Bathsheba. Each of the names is of a person who is either foreign, or immoral, or undesirable, yet (despite or because?) included in the messianic family tree. Redemptive history is inventive and incorporative. It doesn't make any difference who your mother was. Anyone can get into the family. Anyone's personal story can be incorporated into the family history. The purpose of the genealogy is to demonstrate the endless redemptive range of God's ways in his creation.

The modern Hebrew historian, Yehezkel Kaufmann, tells of an old Jewish tradition that held "that the revelation of a messiah would carry with it a revelation also of lost genealogical information."[32] This is immensely suggestive for pastoral work, for pastoral conversation is not only a matter of paying attention to the name as such, and so filling out a sense of identity, but helping persons recognize that their names are included in the family tree: outsiders as they are, unworthy as they feel, they are, nevertheless, in the plot. Their name is written into the messianic line. The total story is of the Messiah, the "Alpha and the Omega [the beginning and the end], who is and who was and who is to come," (Rev. 1:8) but it is a story in which they are among the participants. However minor their parts are, they are never uninteresting and never insignificant.

"Isn't storytelling always a way of searching for one's origin . . . ?"[33] When my origins are certain in God, the implication is strong that my future is also certain in him, and those certainties provide the conditions which encourage me to live by faith in the present. If, via the story, I can experience what it means to be taken seriously, and via the genealogy, can find that my life is part of the story of salvation, I can live with confidence. Having gotten some of the details of my life tied into the clearly narrated ways of salvation history, I no longer have to know the meaning of all the details. If I know that I am part of an existence that has discernible meaning, I don't have to scrupulously figure out the meaning of each feeling, or gesture, or pain. I don't have to know, at any given moment, the whole story if I am convinced that there is a story. The genealogy, in short, by thrusting Ruth and Naomi and Boaz from a pastoral setting into salvation history, shows that this is not a love story into which they accidentally fell but a redemption story that God has been writing for a long time, and will continue writing. All those who have their stories similarly linked up with the stories of others are helped to live by faith. I no longer have to know everything or control everyone around me in order to be convinced that there is meaning and coherence and purpose and goal, for as C.S. Lewis says, "We ride with our backs to the engine. We have no notion what stage in the journey we have reached. . . . a story is precisely the sort of thing that cannot be understood till you have heard the whole of it."[34]

Since the genealogy maintains an emphasis on the *name* at the same time that it fastens attention on *origins* (which also implies destination—if we have ancestors, we also will have descendants), it keeps the personal story from being absorbed in itself. Lovely as Ruth is, intricate as it is, it is not the whole story, even for the people who are in it. When the village women prayed that Ruth would be "like Rachel and Leah," the small domestic world of Bethlehem was set into the mainstream of the theological-historical splendor of God's ways, proclaimed and celebrated in the covenant preaching and praise of worship.

Pastoral work, after collaborating with persons in the making of their stories, leads them back to the vicinity of Pulpit, and Table, and Font, where they discover their faith lineage with Perez in the background and David (and Christ!) ahead. The Christian faith matures only when it is comprehended in the longer perspectives. There is a great deal more to the gospel than individual fulfillment and satisfaction—there is the vast enterprise of the Cross. Back in the sanctuary, while everything continues to be personal, nothing is confined within the limitations of any one person's circumstances.

"What Does This Mean?"

For centuries it was the pastor's defined task to "prepare people for a good death." It is still not an unworthy goal for pastoral work. The true absurdity, though, is not death itself, but the appalling lives so many people lead. When pastors help people tell the stories of their lives, we contribute to a coherent sense of self. These persons become aware that their endeavors and their lives make sense and are meaningful in the actual environments in which they live at that moment. Even in Bethlehem. Pastors who have an unsatisfied hunger for the commonplace whet a similar appetite in others and enable them to find meaning where they least expect it, discover drama behind doors in their own homes and neighborhoods, and perceive a link with salvation in their own parents and children.

Paul Goodman's "little prayer" captures, both in style and content, the "narrative manner" that pastoral work acquires from going to school in the book of Ruth.

> Page after page I have lived Your world
> in the narrative manner, Lord,
>   in my own voice I tell Your story.
>   Needless to say, I envy
>
> people who dramatically
> act the scenes of Your play.
>   Even so, the narrative manner
>   is my *misère et grandeur*.
>
> It is our use
> that some of us
>   insist on how
>   it is from our point of view.[35]

There is no evidence that Ruth was read at the annual Pentecost celebration as early as the first century, A.D.; the first references to that practice do not come until the eighth century, A.D. But on the Day of Pentecost, described in Acts, chapter 2, there was a similar combination of the magnificent and the ordinary that we know took place in later Jewish pastoral tradition when the Ruth story was set alongside the Sinai revelation. That Day of Pentecost when the Holy Spirit descended and formed the assembled worshipers into the Christian church, was every bit as splendid and dramatic as anything that took place at Sinai. But the event was not only public and awesome, it was inward and personal for the "outsiders" who were there (seventeen varieties are listed) reported that they heard "in our own tongues the mighty works of God." (Acts 2:11)

When "the mighty works of God" (the theme of Pentecost) were told "in our own tongues" (the style of Ruth), the church came into being, a community of faith in which the "old, old story" found fresh expression in new stories of obedience and trust, love and blessing. " 'Doesn't listening to a story mean living it as well?' "[36]

The
PASTORAL WORK
of
PAIN-SHARING:
LAMENTATIONS

Suffering is a proof not only of the God-forsakenness of creation but of the depths of being. If there were no suffering in a fallen and sinful world, it would be finally severed from being; the depth of being shows itself in it as suffering. The mystery of existence is revealed in suffering. . . . Suffering is a consequence of sin, a sign of sin, and at the same time redemption from sin and liberation from it. This is the meaning of Christ's suffering on the cross. This is implied in all ideas of a suffering God. Consequently, our attitude to suffering is complex.

Nicolas Berdyaev[1]

Among other things pastoral work is a decision to deal, on the most personal and intimate terms, with suffering. It does not try to find ways to minimize suffering or ways to avoid it. It is not particularly interested in finding explanations for it. It is not a search after the cure for suffering. Pastoral work *engages* suffering. It is a conscious, deliberate plunge into the experience of suffering. The decision has its origin and maintains its integrity in the scriptures which shape pastoral ministry.

The biblical revelation neither explains nor eliminates suffering. It shows, rather, God entering into the life of suffering humanity, accepting and sharing the suffering. Scripture is not a lecture from God, pointing the finger at unfortunate sufferers and saying, "I told you so: here and here and here is where you went wrong; now you are paying for it." Nor is it a program from God providing, step by step, for the gradual elimination of suffering in a series of five-year plans (or, on a grander scale, dispensations). There is no progress from more to less suffering from Egyptian bondage to wilderness wandering, to kingless anarchy, to Assyrian siege, to Babylonian captivity, to Roman crucifixion, to Neronian/Domitian holocaust. The suffering is *there*, and where the sufferer is, God is.

> Surely he has borne our griefs
> and carried our sorrows. (Isa. 53:4)

Pastoral work which finds its definitions and gets its guidelines from an understanding of the way God works, finds in the biblical record an exceedingly clear picture of the ways in which God responds to suffering. It proceeds to use this picture as orientation and perspective for pastoral responses to suffering and comes to see that pastoral work is an assignment to share experiences of suffering.

But it is a tough assignment. Especially since there are culturally sanctioned alternatives which pastors can pursue with neither loss of prestige nor suspicion of defection. In fact, when the alternatives are pursued, there is usually an increase of prestige in the community and a growing admiration in the church. The alternatives are easier, expected (even encouraged) by those who suffer, and are nearly always more lucrative. We work in a culture which is characterized *vis a vis* suffering, by what Philip Rieff calls the "triumph of the therapeutic."[2]

If, in the face of both the human difficulties in engaging in it and the cultural pressures to deviate from it, the biblical-pastoral response is to be maintained, there must be continual nurture at the source. Constant scriptural feedback is required to keep the position sharply delineated and freshly responsive.

Context

Lamentations is a source document eminently suited for such work. In 587 B.C. the holy city Jerusalem fell to Babylonian armies.

The leaders and many of the people were marched six hundred miles away into exile. It was disaster and suffering on a monumental scale: Lamentations is a funeral service for the death of the city.

It is impossible to overstate either the intensity or the complexity of the suffering that resulted from the fall of Jerusalem. Loss was total. Carnage was rampant. Cannibalism and sacrilege were twin horrors stalking the streets of destroyed Jerusalem. The desperate slaying of innocent children showed complete loss of hope in human worth, and the angry murder of priests showed absolute loss of respect for divine will. The worst that can happen to body and spirit, to person and nation, happened here—a nadir of suffering.

> Look, O LORD, and see!
>   With whom hast thou dealt thus?
> Should women eat their offspring,
>   the children of their tender care?
> Should priest and prophet be slain
>   in the sanctuary of the LORD?
>
> In the dust of the streets
>   lie the young and the old;
> my maidens and my young men
>   have fallen by the sword;
> in the day of thy anger thou hast slain them,
>   slaughtering without mercy.
>
> Thou didst invite as to the day of
>   an appointed feast
>   my terrors on every side;
> and on the day of the anger of the LORD
>   none escaped or survived;
> those whom I dandled and reared
>   my enemy destroyed. (2:20–22)

Israel kept the experience of the fall of Jerusalem current in its common life by remembering the event in an annual act of worship —a fast on the Ninth of Ab. The fast uses rituals of penitence to interpret the great judgment as a time of national humiliation and suffering. It was a time for remembering the experience of desolation and reflecting on the realities of divine judgment. The fast was kerygmatic in that it proclaimed with power the God of judgment: God takes sin seriously. When we sin, we have to deal not only with natural consequences (the suffering wrecked by the Babylonian armies) but with divine wrath (God's displeasure and our guilt). Annually, on the Ninth of Ab, the event was remembered and the truth preached. It is in this context that Lamentations directs pastoral ministry.

Lamentations, assigned for reading on the Ninth of Ab, functions as a pastoral ministry by dealing with the suffering in such a way as to direct the despair which ordinarily accompanies guilt *towards* God and not *away from* him. In so doing it defends against the development of an overscrupulous conscience which so often comes from a compulsive concern to please a hard-to-please God. Suffering, in itself, does not lead a person into a deeper relationship with God. It is just as liable to do the opposite, dehumanizing and embittering. The person who experiences suffering can mistakenly interpret the experience as the rejection of God, concluding that because God hates sin, he also hates the sinner. Any religion that takes seriously God's judgment has the pastoral task of realizing God's mercy, demonstrating in a credible way that judgment and mercy are not opposites but complements.

The task of pastoral work is to comfort without in any way avoiding the human realities of guilt or denying the divine realities of judgment. There is no better place for learning how to do that than in the Lamentations. In the midst of suffering Lamentations keeps attention on the God who loves his people so that the judgment does not become impersonal nor the guilt of the people neurotic, nor the misfortune merely general. It pays detailed attention to the exact ways in which suffering takes place; it takes with absolute seriousness the feelings that follow in the wake of judgment; and then it shapes these sufferings and feelings into forms of response to God. Pain thus becomes accessible to compassion. Lamentations develops the pastoral empathies which nurture a saving relationship with the God who wounds and binds up, the God of the cross and the resurrection.

Form

The form of Lamentations is functional, the literary style being as important as its contents. The laments are all composed on an

alphabetic structure as acrostics. The five laments together consti-
tute, in company with Psalm 119, the most elaborate acrostic composition in the Bible. Each of the first four poems is a complete acrostic.
The fifth poem is not acrostic, but its twenty-two lines, correspond-
ing to the number of letters in the Hebrew alphabet, hint at it. In
chapter 3, the center chapter, not only the first, but all three lines
of each strophe, begin with the appropriate letter of the alphabet.

There is no emotion that is more spontaneous, and more individualized, than suffering. How, then, can the highly structured
acrostic be appropriate? How can the artifice of the acrostic serve the
needs of the anguished lament?

The commonest use of the acrostic was to facilitate memory. But
that cannot be the reason for the use here; here it is to guarantee that
the grief and despair are expressed completely.[3] The acrostic patiently, and carefully, goes through the letters of the alphabet and
covers the ground of suffering. Every detail of suffering comes under
consideration.

One of the commonest ways to deal with another's suffering is
to make light of it, to gloss it over, to attempt shortcuts through it.
Because it is so painful, we try to get to the other side quickly.
Lamentations provides a structure to guarantee against that happen-
ing. A regular Talmudic idiom speaks of keeping the Torah from
aleph to tau or, as we would say, from A to Z.[4] Lamentations puts
the idiom to work by being attentive to suffering. It is important to
pay attention to everything that God says; but it is also important to
pay attention to everything that men and women feel, especially
when that feeling is as full of pain and puzzlement as suffering.

The acrostic is a structure for taking suffering seriously. The
endless patience for listening to and paying attention to the suffering
is emphasized in the fact that not only is Lamentations an acrostic—
it *repeats* the acrostic form. It goes over the story again and again and
again and again and again—five times.

The first poem begins by describing what Zion's troubles look
like from the outside:

How lonely sits the city
that was full of people! (1:1)

It ends by crying out what it feels like from the inside:

"Is it nothing to you, all you who pass by?
    Look and see
if there is any sorrow like my sorrow
    which was brought upon me." (1:12)

The cry moves from sympathetic solace to empathetic pain.

The second chapter extends the range of suffering into the area of divine wrath. No emotion is more unpleasant or more difficult to face than anger. When it is God's anger to be faced, the difficulty is enormous. The acrostic pattern maintains a posture of attention: the unthinkable is itemized. The desire to whitewash, to avoid, to euphemize—all these are rejected, and the divine wrath and its consequences in the destroyed city are faced:

How the Lord in his anger
    has set the daughter of Zion under a cloud! (2:1)

The Lord has become like an enemy,
    he has destroyed Israel;
he has destroyed all its palaces,
    laid in ruins its strongholds;
and he has multiplied in the daughter of Judah
    mourning and lamentation. (2:5)

The third chapter intensifies the acrostic by having each line of the three-line strophe begin with the same letter. " '. . . suddenly, in the third place, an individual man appears! After all, an individual is able really to lament most deeply what he has experienced personally. The result is an expression of despair—the third, but this is the deepest.' "[5] It is the most personal of the laments, providing intense individualization:

I am the man who has seen affliction
    under the rod of his wrath. (3:1)

No longer is the lament being conducted from the outside, looking on. Now it is from the inside. The first person singular is used throughout this chapter, except for a brief extension into the plural in vss. 40–47 ("Let us test and examine our ways . . ."). After a few sentences the singular first person is resumed ("my eyes flow with rivers of tears . . ." vs. 48) emphasizing the individual pathos of the concentrated suffering.

The fourth chapter relaxes the intense emotion of the earlier poems and returns to the third person. "The tone is more matter-of-fact."[6] The change of pace is timely. The intensities of chapter 3 cannot be sustained in the human breast. The acrostic device continues to explore the suffering but now from a distance.

> How the gold has grown dim,
>   how the pure gold is changed!
> The holy stones lie scattered
>   at the head of every street (4:1)

Images begin to repeat themselves. Metaphors take on a familiar look. Images of punishment, illness, war, imprisonment, and wild beasts are used to express the complexity and terror of suffering. Putting a name to pain is a first step in recovery from it. The metaphors give handles to the suffering so that it can be grasped and handed over to God.

> Emotion, which is suffering, ceases to be suffering as soon as we form a clear and precise picture of it.[7]

The fifth chapter is a prayer: there have been prayers earlier which have intruded into the lament, but they have not been sustained. The final lament places the entire matter before God. It departs in three ways from the previous laments: it is shorter—only twenty-two lines this time; it is not strictly an acrostic, the a, b, c sequences being dropped—but even here the influence of the acrostic is felt in that there are twenty-two lines for the twenty-two letters of the Hebrew alphabet; and it leaves off the emotionally charged *kinah* meter for the smoother balanced three/three beat of ordinary prayer, "The exhaustion of human possibility clearly presupposes the possibility of God."[8]

In such ways does the acrostic function: it organizes grief, patiently going over the ground, step by step, insisting on the significance of each detail of suffering. The pain is labeled—defined and objectified. Arranged in the acrostic structure the suffering no longer obsesses, no longer controls. The rough rhythm of the *kinah* meter expressing the inner anarchy is patiently arranged in an order which becomes a work of art. Edweena in Thornton Wilder's *Theophilus North* says: " 'The mistakes we make don't really hurt us . . . when we understand every inch of the ground.' "9

The acrostic form of Lamentations demonstrates a pastoral style which develops detailed sympathy and at the same time insists on a termination:

> Weeping may tarry for the night [or a week or six months],
> but joy comes with the morning. (Ps. 30:5)

The acrostic form makes certain that nothing is left out, but it also, just as certainly, puts limits upon the repetitions. If there is a beginning to evil, there is also an end to it. There are only twenty-two letters in the Hebrew alphabet. When you have used them up, you can return to the beginning and start over again, but after you have done that a few times, the realization begins to dawn that that territory has been covered. Sorrow and suffering are not infinite. Any serious discomfort, illness, hurt, or loss seems at the time of impact as if it will go on forever, getting worse all the time. But, in fact, it does not. There is either healing or death. There comes a time when either life ends or the suffering ends. The subjective feeling of endlessness in suffering is, in fact, false. But how is that to be communicated? It does no good to tell a person that it's going to get better tomorrow, or that if he or she just hangs in there long enough, everything will be okay. Lamentations provides a model for dealing with this sense of endlessness in suffering by putting the suffering within the frame of the acrostic. There is a countable, alphabetical scheme—so that when you are at A, you know that Z is, even though a long way off, still there, and that will end the series. The acrostic framework of Lamentations gives a context to the suffering which has boundaries. A sense of finitude is communicated by indirect, nonverbal, means. *Fluant lacrimae, sed eadem et desinant!*—Let the tears flow, but let them also cease!

There are different ways in which pastors do this. The simple act of making an appointment to return to listen again to the tale of tragedy or sorrow or whatever begins to put boundaries around it. Order begins to infiltrate the chaos of the sufferer in the very prosaic act of making another appointment, three to seven days hence. The scheduled appointment written on a calendar, intrudes sequence into the jumbled disarray of a life turned into rubble. The dependable recurrence of times when the ground is gone over and over again shapes forms of wholeness. As much as what is said at such times, the structure for saying it ("the medium is the message") is important.

The acrostic form serves a pastoral function also by communicating a sense of terminus to suffering. There is some reason initially to listen to persons for as long as they want to talk, but probably not more than once. After that, the conversation should be bound by an agreed upon time. Not because the pastor has so many demands that he or she must schedule the time, but because the sorrow must be bound, placed within limits, told within the scheme.

There is no question in Lamentations about not taking suffering seriously. Every permutation of suffering is attended to. Every line of pain is traced in patient detail. Finally, though, it says "Enough." Evil is not inexhaustible. It is not infinite. It is not worthy of a lifetime of attention.

Timing is important. If a terminus is proposed too soon, people know that their suffering has not been taken seriously and conclude that it is therefore without significance. But if it goes on too long, the pastor becomes an accessory to neurotic responses, a crippled adjustment to life which frustrates wholeness. "To some, ill health is a way to be important."[10]

This insight is a pastoral necessity if evil is to be taken seriously as well as kept in control. There are biblical themes repeated in Genesis, Job, The Psalms, and Isaiah regarding the ordering of chaos. The Babylonian monster Rahab (or *Tiamat*) thrashes across the heavens and churns the ocean deeps but is finally put in its place —chained (Rev. 20:1–3). Evil is recognized and bravely faced, but it is not permitted to become an obsession. There is an end to concerns about it. Ministry to the sufferer must establish the significance of what is suffered; it must not concede its ultimacy.

History

For a document so full of intense emotion it is remarkable (and important) that at all times Lamentations is also in touch with history.

Nothing in scripture has so much feeling in it as Lamentations, but all the feelings can be traced to actual facts. "The linking of the poems of Lamentations with the events of 587 is well established."[11] Suffering is not a surrealist nightmare; it comes out of materials that can be described in sober prose and discussed by ordinary folk. Trouble occurs in a locatable place and at a datable time.

In Lamentations the feelings are intense but the facts are firm. Each feeling is riveted to a fact, which means that the suffering at no time is allowed to become *mere* feeling. The anguish is never given an independent existence. Norman Gottwald has carefully documented eleven historical episodes described in the 2 Kings 25 narrative of the Fall of Jerusalem that can also be discerned in the Lamentations. At no time do the laments depart from the factual realities of 2 Kings: the siege; the famine; the flight of the king; the looting of the temple; the burning of the temple, palace, and important buildings; the demolitions of the city walls; the slaughter of the leaders; the exile of the inhabitants; the expectation, then collapse of foreign help; Judah's fickle political allies; the provincial status of Judah.[12]

The function, though, of 2 Kings 25 in relation to Lamentations is not to explain but to locate suffering, for if suffering is severed from historical data, it diffuses, filling up the room like gas.

Names, places, buildings, dates are ways of tethering suffering, holding it within the framework of history. Suffering assumes its place as one among other things. It is not everything. It is not the whole world. It is not an entire history. No suffering is more monumental than the Fall of Jerusalem; still, it took place in a single year, in a sequence of events that comprises eleven items. The consequences exceed that calendar year, of course, but not infinitely. There were centuries of history previous to Jerusalem's fall, and there would be centuries of history after it. Abraham and Moses were in the background, and Messiah was in the future. Lamentations is a historical event, not a cosmic condition.

When a pastor encounters a person in trouble, the first order of pastoral ministry is to enter into the pain and to share the suffering. Later on the task develops into clearing away the emotional rubble and exposing the historical foundations: all suffering is triggered by something. There is a datable event behind an act of suffering—a remembered word of scorn which wounded, a describable injustice causing injury, a death with a date on it pinpointing the hour of loss, a divorce decree giving legal definition to a rejection. Suffering explodes in a life, and pain is scattered like shrapnel. At the moment the loss seems total, but gradually it is possible to recognize and touch many, many things, persons, areas that remain sound and stable—to discover weakness, to admit guilt, to accept responsibility, to be grateful for survival. But if we fail to maintain a foothold in local history, suffering like a helium-filled balloon lifts us off the ground, and we drift, directionless, through the air at the mercy of emotional air currents and the barometric pressures of hormonal secretions. Sorrow that does not have historical ballast becomes anxiety and turns finally into mental illness or emotional bitterness History is necessary, not to explain, but to anchor.

The reason for exposing the substratum of history in Lamentations and insisting on uncovering it in each individual instance of suffering is that deliverance (for which the sufferer hopes and the pastor prays) is always and everywhere a historical phenomenon. It never takes place outside history—not in a mystical trance, not in a gnostic enlightenment. All kerygma is historical: the Exodus from Egypt, the theophany at Sinai, the conquest of Canaan, the enthronement on Zion, the birth at Bethlehem, the crucifixion on Calvary, the empty tomb, the Pentecostal languages. If suffering is divorced from its history, it will not be easy to hear the kerygmatic message. The Bible does not deduce redemption from a myth of primeval innocence but from the Egyptian Exodus in 1250 B.C., nor is judgment referred to an apocalyptic holocaust but accepted in the Jerusalem fall in 587 B.C. The result is that God's acts of mercy are discovered in both events and permeate the ordinary days of the people of God.

There is, it is true, a sense in which persons suffer simply because we are human: "Man is born to trouble as the sparks fly upward." The Fall of Adam and Eve has resulted in bruises and injuries that continue to afflict their descendants. But in specific instances of suffering—a death, a depression, a separation, a rejection—it is possible to develop a sense of actual, local, personal history. In Lamentations it is the Fall of Jerusalem, not the Fall of Adam, that is behind the laments. It is not the general fallen condition of humankind which brought about this weeping but the specific siege, famine, rapes, and murders of the Babylonian invasion. Separated from its history, suffering swells out of proportion to its cause. Abstracted from events, suffering develops either intellectual vagaries (problem of pain philosophies) or emotional trouble in the form of "out of touch" psychoses. Trouble severed from history becomes self-indulgent. A painful feeling (any feeling for that matter) cut off from its environment, loses touch with reality and develops all the symptoms of the emotionally disturbed or the aesthetically decadent.

So the observation that the poetry of the Lamentations is constantly working on the stuff of history is useful to pastoral work. Von Rad writes: "Poetry—especially with the peoples of antiquity—is much more than an aesthetic pastime: rather is there in it a penetrating desire for knowledge directed towards the data presented by the historical and natural environment."[13] Von Rad's insight is cogent to Lamentations: here we do not find suffering persons "expressing themselves," making beautiful art out of a horrible experience. The laments are a search for redemption roots in the devastations of judgment.

Pastoral immersion in the history-soaked lines of Lamentations is defense and protection against all a-historical therapies which are made available for pastoral use. The "primal scream" therapy of Janov is typical of these so-called therapies. Janov and his numerous imitators provide the setting and encouragement for the sufferer to vent the accumulated anger and resentment and hurt piled up in layer after layer of pain in the personality. Dionysiac emotion explodes like thunder and lightening in a summer storm. Then the sun comes out and the birds sing. A wonderful feeling of well-being ensues. There is catharsis. But there is no healing—there cannot be, for no respect or attention was given to the facts of suffering: places, names, dates. A friend, overwhelmed by personal, marital, and vocational troubles began going to New York City for "scream" weekends. The results were wonderful—and lasted anywhere from two to seven days. I said to him at one point, "Why don't you shut yourself up in a room with Lamentations and Isaiah

53 for a weekend?" He looked at me uncomprehendingly.

It would, though, have been far healthier, if more exacting. Lamentations takes second-place to no one in its ability to evoke and face the emotions of suffering. Every ugly, difficult, painful emotion is there and expressed with cathartic power. But there is also personal history. Every line of Lamentations can be footnoted from 2 Kings 25. There is an acceptance of the stuff that makes up the ordinary in life: places and dates, events and decisions. It cries its pain under the same conditions in which God works his salvation—"under Pontius Pilate" and "on the third day." If the *poetry* of suffering is separated from the *prose* of suffering, it is cut off from the place where God does his work and is mere emotive impulse, aestheticism gone to seed.

When a pastor asks, "What happened?" (after having asked "How do you feel?") it is not in order to minimize suffering, or to "put it in perspective." It is, rather, to pin it to the actual and so make it accessible to the grace which operates, as we know from biblical accounts, in the historical. In addition to participating in the sorrow, the pastor makes connections with the everyday realities of what has happened, combining empathy with confrontation, compassion with witness.

Anger

If, at one level, Lamentations is an immersion in human suffering, at another level it is an encounter with God's anger. The anger of God is referred to continuously through the laments, and faced with neither apology nor self-pity (1:12; 2:1; 2:2; 2:3; 2:6; 2:21; 2:22; 3:1; 3:43; 3:66; 4:11; 5:22). "The richness and variety of the Old Testament vocabulary for wrath has often been noted, and this book utilizes the full range of expressions."[14]

The effectiveness of Lamentations as ministry in the area of suffering is in no small measure due to the resoluteness, throughout, in dealing with the anger of God.

One of the commonest ways to account for suffering is with the tossed-off phrase "That's the way things are," or "That's the way the ball bounces." Such phrases attribute suffering to a basic impersonalism at the foundation. Life is invaded by brute, dumb, and demonic forces. There is no accounting for them. They are irrational and unpredictable—but they are there and must be put up with. Lamentations is a distillation of the biblical view that when we suffer, we experience something intensely personal—the anger of God. The use of anger to describe something in God means that we are dealing with what can be comprehended from the stuff of our own experience. At the same time, though, that this leads to a profound and hopeful understanding of suffering, it opens the door to possible misunderstanding.

As for the misunderstanding, our experience of anger is often with its neurotic forms. We have only occasional encounters with mature, healthy anger. Anger as an honest manifestation of revealed love, or offended righteousness, is rare among us. We encounter it mostly as a kind of petty irritation, a tantrum, a mean streak coming out when we don't get our own way.

[margin note: healthy anger]

But even among mortals there are times when anger is majestic and whole: a pouring out of moral concern, a rousing to passionate response, a *caring.* When it does, while we can hardly be comfortable in its presence, we know that we are dealing with the personal, the intentional, the righteous, and the free.

The Hebrew fondness for using anger to describe something in God derives from this understanding. God's anger, among the Hebrews, was always evidence of his concern: "God's concern is the prerequisite and source of His anger. It is because He cares for man that His anger may be kindled against man."[15] God

> is . . . moved and affected by what happens in the world, and reacts accordingly. Events and human actions arouse in Him joy or sorrow, pleasure or wrath. He is not conceived as judging the world in detachment. He reacts in an intimate and subjective manner and thus determines the value of events.[16]

Those who would bowdlerize the Bible by expurgating all references to God's anger hardly know what they are doing. They have not thought through the consequences of their "improvements." The moment anger is eliminated from God, suffering is depersonalized, for anger is an insistence on the personal—it is the antithesis of impersonal fate or abstract law.

In our technological culture we have a great fondness for mechanical analogies and impersonal abstractions. C. S. Lewis who thought as long and as deeply about these things as anyone in our century once wrote that our attempt to explain suffering by substituting the idea that we have tangled with a "live wire" rather than angered our King was worse than foolish. The substitution of impersonal, mechanical analogies for personal, hierarchical ones is a net loss. "What do you suppose you have gained by substituting the image of a live wire for that of an angered majesty? You have shut us all up in despair; for the angry king can forgive, and electricity can't."[17] Karl Barth gives similar testimony: ", . . whenever men apprehend their misery as having been prepared for them by God and their guilt as wrong done to Him, and when in consequence there is for them no other hope but God—then there is opened up the possibility which can never be locked against them."[18]

The last sentence in Lamentations is blunt and direct: ". . . hast thou utterly rejected us? Art thou exceedingly angry with us?" (5:22) But this anger is addressed in the most personal of relationships, prayer. Prayer is suffering's best result. In prayer, God's anger is neither sentimentally glossed nor cynically debunked, but seized as a lever to pry open the door of redemption. The sufferer, by praying, does not ask God to think well of him or her, but asks that God will enact redemption, working "fruits meet for repentence" through Jesus Christ who suffered and died for all.

If suffering is conceived as impersonal or abstract, it sends us to the philosophers for a "metaphysic of evil," or to the theologians for a theodicy, or to the psychologists for a diagram of the unconscious. But suffering which is understood under the rubric of God's anger provokes understanding and releases insight into what it means to be a responsible person of faith. Clearly, this is what happens in Lamentations. What the people had supposed in the days of their prosperity to have been harmless peccadilloes is seen in the desolation of the Jerusalem Fall to be grievous sin. Jackals prowling through the ruined Temple precincts of Zion (5:18) are evidence of a gross evil which had insinuated itself quietly and unobstrusively into the life of God's people. The sight of the sins, for decades hidden in the heart but now open in the streets, provokes repentance: "woe to us, for we have sinned!" (5:16) Our very pain is a sign of God's remembrance of us, for it would be much worse if we were left in ghastly isolation. "Be thankful," counseled P. T. Forsyth, "that God cares enough for you to be angry with you."[19] Anger uses the material of suffering to intensify the relationship of love. It breaks through indifference. It smashes through apathy. It confounds abstractions. It insists that God personally deal with free persons who are capable of rising above despair into repentance, into faith, into hope. The words for "enemy" and "lover" differ in Hebrew by only one letter ('ahb, 'ayb). Lamentations 1:5, "her enemies prosper" is only a consonant away from Psalm 122:6, "They shall prosper that love Thee." (See also Lamentations 2:5–10, author's translation.)

The concept of God's anger imparts to suffering a hueristic quality: here is stimulus to discover the personal in God, the caring in God, the compassion in God. Abraham Heschel is passionate in his insight:

> Agony is the final test. When all hopes are dashed and all conceit is shattered, man begins to miss what he has long spurned. In darkness, God becomes near and clear. "He shall go through it suffering and hungry, and then when hungry he shall break out in anger and curse his king and his gods; He shall turn his face upwards, and look upon the earth, and behold distress and darkness. But there will be no gloom for her that was in anguish. . . . The people that walked in darkness behold a great light; those who dwelt in a land of deep darkness, on them a light shines" (Isa. 8:21–9:2 . . .).
> When all pretensions are abandoned, one begins to feel the burden of guilt. It is easier to return from an extreme distance than from the complacencey of a good conscience, from spurious proximity.[20]

The pastor, by virtue of leadership in the worshiping community, is the "visible correlative" of the God known through history as Redeemer. The pastor's participation in the circumstances of suffering in acts of visitation and consultation becomes a referent by which a person transmutes what feels absurd to what is proclaimed as significant.

The single most important observation that comes out of an examination of biblical references to the anger of God is "The consistent linking of nouns for wrath with Yahweh, the covenant God [which] is of supreme theological significance. It shows that the idea of wrath is closely bound up with belief in the covenant."[21] This is the new factor in Israel, in contrast with the conceptions held in common in the ancient East. Rooted and defended by the experience at Sinai, all God's dealings with the people are seen in terms of maintenance of the covenant, and so the experience of divine wrath is connected with covenant violations. God's anger is not incalculable or arbitrary—it takes place within a clearly defined, well-known structure. The story of God's salvation was often told. The ways of the covenant God were rehearsed in hymn and ritual. "There can never be any question of despotic caprice striking out in blind rage."[22] The people, even in their most desperate straits, with the help of pastoral ministries such as those represented in Lamentations understand God certainly via the covenant, not uncertainly as a brute demonic power.

We sometimes say to a person who is easily offended, "Don't take it personally." Pastoral ministry brings a different message, namely, "Take it personally." Suffering is the intensification of what is personal: the importance of pastoral work here is double. First, it provides a context in which suffering is experienced against the immense backdrop of a majestic salvation. Pastoral work weaves a tapestry of the threads *rahum ve-hannun*, "merciful and gracious" (Exod. 34:6; Ps. 86:15; 103:8), or *hannun ve-rahum* (Joel 2:13; Jonah 4:2; Pss. 111:4; 112:4; 116:5; 145:8; Neh. 9:17,31; 2 Chron. 30:9). There are qualities which are never separable in the Bible from the concept of God. His anger passes, his love goes on forever. "I have loved you with an everlasting love." (Jer. 31:3) "I will betroth you to me for ever . . . in . . . love, and in mercy." (Hosea 2:19) Again and again we are told that God's love or kindness *(hesed)* goes on forever (Jer. 33:11; Pss. 100:5; 106:1; 107:1; 118:1–4; 136:1–26; Ezra 3:11). We are never told that his anger goes on forever.

Second, pastoral work, having demonstrated a personal relationship with a covenant God who is merciful and gracious, goes on to provide an immediate companionship. Pastors accompany persons in meeting and dealing with God's anger, encountering it, accepting the pain, and submitting to its influences in evoking repentance, if need be, and faith, always. That companionship assures the continuity of God's concern and convinces the sufferer that God's wrath is not an emotional outburst or an irrational fit, but an aspect of his persevering care. Pastoral work joins the sufferer, shares the experience of God's anger, enters into the pain, the hurt, the sense of absurdity, the descent into the depths. It is not the task of the pastor to alleviate suffering, to minimize it, or to mitigate it, but to share it after the example of our Lord Messiah: "Surely he hath borne our griefs, and carried our sorrows." (Isa. 53:4 K.J.V.) By doing that, the pastor assists a person to intensify a capacity for suffering, enable a person to "lean into the pain,"[23] to "rend the veil that lies between life and pain."[24]

Pastoral work that avoids doing that demits ministry among the suffering. The pastor who substitutes cheery bromides for this companionship "through the valley of deep shadows" can fairly be accused of cowardice. Writing cheerful graffiti on the rocks in the valley of deep shadows is no substitute for companionship with the person who must walk in the darkness. John Updike describes his famous everyman, Rabbit Angstrom, thus:

> Harry has no taste for the dark, tangled, visceral aspect of Christianity, the *going through* quality of it, the passage *into* death and suffering that redeems and inverts these things, like an umbrella blowing inside out. He lacks the mindful will to walk the straight line of a paradox. His eyes turn toward the light however it glances into his retina.[25]

The gospel that boldly sets the cross of Christ at the center of its message, also courageously accepts the cross of discipleship as part of its daily routines. Difficulties and suffering are not problems for which the gospel provides an escape, but part of a reality which the Christian experiences and in which Christians share a faith by encouraging one another in hope. Pastoral work articulates and exhibits this mutual support.

Pastoral work in suffering is like a Jacobean wrestling with the angel at Peniel: "I will not let you go till you tell me your name." Pastors grapple with the dark assailants and demand they cough up their meaning. In the dawn, although Jacob walks with a limp, he walks with purpose, with meaning, with integrity. A wounded healer.[26] The night at Peniel held despair before God and confidence in God in a tight embrace. With the morning there came a blessing.

Dignity

Nothing contrasts pastoral work and the humanist traditions more clearly than their respective responses to suffering. The modern humanist traditions see suffering as a deficiency—usually under the analogy of sickness. Something has gone wrong, and a therapist is called in to set it right. Some of this is merely modern: it is the kind of thing Ivan Illich objects to when he argues that there is an American myth that denies suffering and the sense of pain. We act as if they *should* not be, and hence we devalue the *experience* of suffering. But this myth denies our encounter with reality.[27] The approach is to find the cause of the suffering and to eliminate it, either through psychoanalysis, or through environmental change, or social political reform. Suffering, as such, has no value and no meaning—it is only a sign that things have gone wrong, and a challenge to humanity to set them right again through goodwill and ingenuity.

The impact of the clinical pastoral training movement (since Boisen) is ambiguous in its influence at this point. On the positive side it has taught pastors to pay scrupulous attention to each instance of suffering, to bring an intelligent compassion to the event of hurt. It has given proper warnings against the futility of moralizing. But on the negative side, it has encouraged the use of secular, medical models for understanding suffering, and therefore has perpetrated the myth of the therapeutic.[28] Instead of attributing the suffering to the "sins of the fathers," it has assigned them to the neuroses of the mothers, and has put a whole generation of pastors to work in eliminating suffering from the soul. Nothing has been gained and much lost by substituting psychological presuppositions for theological understandings.

Pastors have been herded into the temple shrines of psychiatry, trained in its incantations and rituals, and then sent back into Christian churches to try to practice what they have learned. They have been put in hospitals and clinics as "chaplains," made to sit at the feet of a medical priesthood, in order to learn the cure of souls. Awed by the prestige, the salaries, the vast technology, and the immense power of the medical elite, they return to their parishes thoroughly convinced of their inferiority to the practitioners of modern science. They are sentenced by ordination to live among the suffering in awkward amateurism, mumbling prayers, and handing out prescriptive scriptures, while their superiors scientifically titrate drugs and sell advice with an arrogance unrivaled since the days of the Greek sophists (against whom Socrates railed and fumed).

Pastors have been told by the clinical pastoral training people that they are a part of a "healing team" with physicians and nurses. The statement is a barefaced lie: pastors are barely tolerated nuisances. With only rare exceptions, they are considered aliens. And ought to be. For both their presuppositions and goals are different.

James Otis Sargent Huntington (d. 1935), an American in the Anglican high church tradition of Pusey and Keble, a highly skilled writer of letters of spiritual counsel, excised all utilitarianism from his consolation: " 'Try to live up to the dignity of this suffering.' "[29]

The pastor who accepts this work will neither attempt explanations of suffering nor mount programs for the elimination of it. One of the most offensive phrases to appear in recent literature of pastoral care is "grief management." To attempt to use the techniques of bureaucracy with people at their most human and most vulnerable time and to suppose that with psychological tricks and learned manipulation the pain of death can be reduced or the sorrow of loss be mitigated is simply insensitive.

Pastors have no business interfering with another's sorrow, or manipulating it. Suffering is an event in which we are particularly vulnerable to grace, able to recognize dimensions in God and depths in the self. To treat it as a *"problem"* is to demean the person. The fact that in the Lamentations (in the Bible!) there is no recourse to incantation or magical compulsion to secure protection against the effects of divine anger, a common practice in neighboring civilizations, is warning against the acquisition of "techniques" to alleviate suffering. Lamentations is not grief management. It does, though, by sharing the suffering, help. But it doesn't solve it; it doesn't eliminate it. And it doesn't try. Suffering is a task on which it does not turn its back.

Most people who deal with suffering, pastors prominent among them, are by training and temperament doers and fixers. They want to do something about what is wrong with the world. Suffering is something wrong with a person—and they are prepared to do something about it. But

> . . . suffering is not always a pathological phenomenon; rather than being a symptom of neurosis, suffering may well be a human achievement, especially if the suffering grows out of existential frustration. I would strictly deny that one's search for a meaning to his existence, or even his doubt of it, in every case is derived from, or results in, any disease.[30]

Edith Weisskopf-Joelson observes that " 'our current mental-hygiene philosophy stresses the idea that people ought to be happy, that unhappiness is a symptom of maladjustment. Such a value system might be responsible for the fact that the burden of unavoidable unhappiness is increased by unhappiness about being unhappy.' " She calls for someone to " '. . . counteract certain unhealthy trends in the present-day culture of the United States, where the incurable sufferer is given very little opportunity to be proud of his suffering and to consider it ennobling rather than degrading . . .' "[31]

In counteracting the trend, Lamentations provides demonstrations for the ennoblement of suffering. It *faces* suffering, *encounters* suffering. It doesn't *do* anything about it. It doesn't *give* an answer. It doesn't *provide* a remedy. By taking suffering seriously it gives significance to it. C. S. Lewis puts it this way: "It appears, from all the records, that though He has often rebuked us and condemned us, He has never regarded us with contempt. He has paid us the intolerable compliment of loving us, in the deepest, most tragic, most inexorable sense."[32]

Lamentations stands as a counterforce to the "triumph of the therapeutic." It grounds pastoral work in the painful, patient facing of suffering which is an unavoidable part of the task, without trying to "help." It counters the tendencies to manipulate and alleviate, which are always condescending and in some way or other dehumanizing. By rooting the pastor in a way of taking suffering seriously, it encourages the "longsuffering" of pastoral work, gives meaning and dignity to the person who suffers, and leaves the healing up to God in Christ on the cross.

Encouraged by Lamentations, the pastor will have the strength to *do* far less in relation to suffering, and *be* far more. Pastors will not give in to the temptation to fix the sufferer and will engage in a ministry which honors the sufferer. Nothing, in the long run, does more to demean the person who suffers than to condescendingly busy oneself in fixing him or her up, and nothing can provide more meaning to suffering than a resolute and quiet faithfulness in taking the suffering seriously and offering a companionship through the time of waiting for the morning.

Community

Hermann Gunkel's 1929 analysis of the five poems in Lamentations shows that chapters 1, 2, 4, 5, are all communal laments. Chapter 3 is an individual lament with some communal elements mixed in.[33] Refinements have been made on this general form-critical analysis, but the basic observation stands—Lamentations is communal. Suffering is made into a community act. Whatever individual elements there are (like chapter 3) get incorporated into the lamentations of the community. This is not only true of Lamentations, it is the biblical style. When biblical people wept, they wept with their friends.

This is an important consideration in pastoral work. One of the strategies of pastoral work is to enter private grief and make a shared event of it. The biblical way to deal with suffering is to transform what is individual into something corporate. No single person's sin produced the sufferings consequent to Jerusalem's Fall, and no single person ought to mourn them: response to suffering is a function of the congregation.

Most cultures show a spontaneous comprehension of this. The suffering person is joined by friends who join their tears and prayers in a communal lament. They do not hush up the sound of weeping but augment it. They do not hide the sufferer away from view but bring him or her out into the public square in full view of everyone. The opening scene in Book XXIII of the *Iliad* is typical of ancient cultures. Achilles, who has been skulking down by the boats by himself for most of the battle, is brought upon the scene into the situation in which his best friend, Patroclus, has been killed in battle with the Trojan champion, Hector. Instead of going off by himself to nurse his grief, as he had done earlier to indulge his wounded vanity, he enlists the entire Aechean army in the work of lamentation:

> Chariot-skirmishers, friends of my heart, we'll not unharness our good horses now but in our war-cars filing near Patroklos mourn him in line. That is fit honor paid to a captain fallen. When we've gained relief in lamentation, we can free the teams and take our evening meal here.[34]

When private grief is integrated into communal lament, several things take place. For one thing the act of suffering develops significance. If others weep with me, there must be more to the suffering than my own petty weakness or selfish sense of loss. When others join the sufferer, there is "consensual validation" that the suffering means something. The community votes with its tears that there is suffering that is worth weeping over.

Further, community participation insures a human environment. The threat of dehumanization to which all pain exposes us—of being reduced to the level of "the beasts that perish"—is countered by the presence of other persons whose humanity is unmistakable. The person who, through stubbornness or piety, insists on grieving privately not only depersonalizes him or herself but robs the community of participation in what necessarily expands its distinctiveness as a human community as over against the mob.

Again, when the community joins in the lament, sanction is given for the expression of loss—the outpouring of emotion is legitimized in such a way as to provide for catharsis and then renewal. "Catharsis of grief and rejection is the aim of lament liturgies."[35] The "inability to mourn" (the title of a book by A. and M. Mitscherlich, a study of the widespread "psychic numbing" in Europe following World War II) is a psychiatric problem among those who have no community, leading to devitalization and depression. When suffering cannot be expressed emotionally, there is a consequent inability to recover. A comic/tragic passage in Gunter Grass' post-World War

II novel, *The Tin Drum,* describes this inability to mourn which is pervasive in cultures where community life is attenuated, the desperate attempts to produce tears, and what a depersonalized society must do to compensate for loss:

> for it is not true that when the heart is full the eyes necessarily overflow, some people can never manage it, especially in our century, which in spite of all the suffering and sorrow will surely be known to posterity as the tearless century. It was this drought, this tearlessness that brought those who could afford it to Schmuh's Onion Cellar, where the host handed them a little chopping board —pig or fish—a paring knife for eighty pfennigs, and for twelve marks an ordinary field-, garden-, and kitchen-variety onion, and induced them to cut their onions smaller and smaller until the juice —what did the onion juice do? It did what the world and the sorrows of the world could not do: it brought forth a round, human tear. It made them cry.[36]

Pastoral work cannot adequately function if it is limited to private comfort and individual consolation. The neighbors must be brought into the room; the congregation must gather so that the sufferers come to realize that the pain they cannot resign themselves to is understood by others. Lament and protest can then be placed before God in common prayer. By using the set forms of communal lament at such times, persons who suffer join those paradigmatic sufferers upon whom has come not merely this or that suffering, but the ultimate elemental suffering, and they are able to enter the invisible company of those who have had similar or the same sufferings, and who have survived—who have more than survived—who have been exalted.[37]

Elie Weisel, who has experienced, understood, and given exposition to the twentieth century's suffering puts this pastoral admonition on the lips of a character in his novel, *Gates of the Forest:*

> "It's inhuman to wall yourself up in pain and memories as if in prison. Suffering must open us to others. It must not cause us to reject them. The Talmud tells us that God suffers with man. Why? In order to strengthen the bonds between creation and Creator; God chooses to suffer in order to better understand man and be better understood by him. But you, you insist upon suffering alone. Such suffering shrinks you, diminishes you. Friend, that is almost cruel."[38]

Pastoral work among the suffering wears a path between home and sanctuary—listens to the poured out, individualized grief and brings it into the sanctuary where it becomes part of the common grief, is placed at the foot of the cross and subjected to the powers of salvation which are diagrammed in all theologies of the atonement.

Pastoral work thus brings into every sanctuary what Miguel Unamuno wished would take place in all the streets:

> I am convinced that we should solve many things if we all went out into the streets and uncovered our griefs, which perhaps would prove to be but one sole common grief, and be joined together in beweeping them . . . A *miserere* sung in common by a multitude tormented by destiny has much value as a philosophy. It is not enough to cure the plague; we must learn to weep for it . . . Perhaps that is the supreme wisdom.[39]

Comfort

Everyone who has been ill, or in grief, or hurt, has experienced another's attempts to help—and knows how frequently the attempts are bungled. In a hospital bed, depressed, and in pain, we are not helped by the bright, plastic cheerfulness of pastor or friend who tells us to cheer up for "everything is going to be ok." We already know, in the moments when we are inclined to think about it, that everything is going to be all right (or else know that it is not), but at that moment it would help if there were someone patient and courageous enough simply to share what we are going through—give us the great honor of paying attention to us, treating us as a significant person just as we are. The worst things about loss and hurt are the loneliness and rejection involved in them. That loss cannot be made up for by happy homilies. Erik Routley wrote:

> I heard with some pleasure a sardonic remark from a distinguished minister who was speaking at a university mission, "When I meet some radiant Christians", he said, "I am convinced of the case for the morose Christian." There can be something dreadfully heartless about eupeptic Christianity.[40]

The great Corinthian phrase, "in him it is always Yes," (2 Cor. 1:19) is the foundational cheerfulness basic to all pastoral work. But if it is inappropriately expressed it can only be felt as heartlessness, a failure to take suffering seriously.

Lamentations is insurance against premature comfort, against "healing the wounds of my people lightly." During the time of ruin there are always those who attempt to cover the wounds of judgment with band-aid comfort. But comfort cannot function apart from a serious grappling with the pain of judgment. How many times were the Lamentations said and sung before there rose from the lips of another prophet the new words?

> Comfort, comfort my people, says your God.
> Speak tenderly to Jerusalem,
>   and cry to her
> that her warfare is ended,
>   that her iniquity is pardoned,
> that she has received from the LORD's hand
>   double for all her sins. (Isa. 40:1–2)

Every healer, every pastor, must be alert to the dangers of premature comfort. Denise Levertov's caution is pastoral:

> Yet the fear nags me: is the wound
> my life has suffered
>   healing too fast,
> shutting in bad blood?
> Will the scar
> pucker the skin of my soul?[41]

A pastor who takes an apprenticeship in Lamentations acquires a certain leisure in a ministry with sufferers—one cannot *rush* through an acrostic. In that leisure there will be a chance to develop the patience that takes the details of pain seriously, and thereby imparts a kind of dignity to them.

In the process we will learn that ruins are not disasters: we no longer panic in the face of ruin. One cannot hurry healing. Suffering in Lamentations is not an ominous disaster to be avoided but a difficult, healing operation to be accepted. Debilitating and degrading sins, both ours and others', are dealt with so that the wholeness of redemption restores meaning to all of life. In judgment God tears out the sins that defile devotion, forgives the sins that divide fellowship, and atones for the sins that damn to perdition.

Most of Lamentations is—lamentations. But not all of it. In the center of the laments there is a pool of light: pain's chaos gives way to God-faithfulness which shows salvation lines in the shape of creation.

> I remember my miserable wandering, the wormwood and poison.
> Within myself I surely remember, and am despondent.
> Yet one thing I will keep in mind which will give me hope:
>
> Yahweh's mercy is surely not at an end, nor is his pity exhausted.
> It is new every morning. Great is your faithfulness!
> Yahweh is my portion, I tell myself, therefore I will hope.
> (3.19–24)[47]

The great phrase here is "Yahweh is my portion," a quote from the Torah. Centuries earlier the Lord had said it, and Levi had accepted it (Deut. 10:9; Num. 18:20). The promise had been preserved. The ancient phrase had been handed down through many generations, held onto tenaciously through the worst of troubles. And then, suddenly, under the pressure of suffering, it all at once released quite unexpected contents. *Pathemata mathemata* ("suffered things are learned things"). Now the people knew that there was a communion with a merciful God which could not be lost because it could not be touched by the dislocations of external circumstance.

Through the racking anarchic sobs of the *kinah* meter the kerygmatic sentences are whispered (or trumpeted!). The chaos and darkness of suffering become first-day light. "Yahweh's mercy is surely not at an end, nor is his pity exhausted. It is new every morning. Great is your faithfulness!" A genesis word. Nietzsche wrote the epigram: " 'Only where graves are, is there resurrection.' "[43]

The
PASTORAL WORK
of
NAY-SAYING:
ECCLESIASTES

A man may be of value to another man, not because he wishes to be important, not because he possesses some inner wealth of soul, not because of something he is, but because of what he is—not. His importance may consist in his poverty, in his hopes and fears, in his waiting and hurrying, in the direction of his whole being towards what lies beyond his horizon and beyond his power. The importance of an apostle is negative rather than positive. In him a void becomes visible. And for this reason he is something to others: he is able to share grace with them, to focus their attention, and to establish them in waiting and in adoration.

—Karl Barth[1]

Pastoral work takes place in a crowded religious fair, noisy with the bargaining of shoppers and hawkers—those who have ventured out in the hope of finding something that will make their lives better, and those who promise that they have something that will make life better.

The shoppers expect to receive something that they could not otherwise get on their own and to learn something that they could not discover by themselves. They expect to get in on something that transcends the natural, and to understand something that exceeds the mundane. The ordinary term for what they expect is "god." And they expect the pastor to give it to them.

"God" even for those who have only the haziest of concepts and engage in only the most muddled thinking, is known to be more than human, both in power and wisdom, in what he does and what he knows. God works in ways beyond our capacities. God speaks in ways that surpass our understanding. So far, the definition, however much other ignorance is mixed into it, is reasonably accurate.

Since "no one has seen God at any time" and the pastor is perfectly visible at most times, the expectations that people have of God are often focused on the pastor, the bull's-eye for God-targeted expectations. The expectations converge from a wide horizon: moral idealism, spiritual hunger, evidence of righteousness, advocacy for justice, rewards for being good, answers to enigmas. What people, informed by the grapevine of religion, are looking for is aimed at the pastor.

As such, the pastor is in an enviable position. Our daily work crisscrosses routines in people's lives where they are most open to and expectant of eternity. The ordinary parish constitutes something of what Henry James called "the enormous lap of the actual"—and in that "lap" the pastor tells the stories, models the love, and administers the nourishment that proclaim and realize God's redemptive love for his people. The fact that what people want from God is quite often wrong and what they expect from God silly   that is, that their expectations have only a dubious relation to their real needs and to God's revealed will—is not, in itself, a serious problem. At least they want something more than what they have been able to get and think on their own: they are open to something beyond and above; and they have come to a person of integrity and training for assistance. If the pastor has first to develop self-understanding among the parishioners so that personal needs are conceived more accurately, and needs to teach what Jesus so very clearly and plainly made known of God's nature so that the divine will is comprehended soundly, that is no more than he or she should expect, living in a post-Eden world. In this context a pastor is able to work patiently and persistently, confident that when pastoral counsel and proclamation are sound, persons who are serious about their life with God will finally receive the salvation/wholeness that they need.

But the enviableness of the pastor's position palls no little bit when we realize that we are not the only ones to whom people come for help in completing God-related expectations. We work on a street teeming with competition. Every kind of religious leadership is offered to persons who want "god." No pastor is provided the luxury of people's exclusive attention. Congregations are not sequestered between Sundays from religious propaganda and spiritual promises, from the radio message and the television spectacular, newspaper advice and magazine wisdom. "Religious" counsel and "gospel" preaching pour into the mind at an unprecedented rate. St. Paul, angry at schismatic itinerants who were unsettling his congregations with gaudy but cheap doctrines, faced only a fraction of what today's pastor gets from the competitors, many of whom have access to the expensive mass media.

So pastoral work takes place in a context in which every kind of spiritual expectation is directed to the pastor (which is encouraging): it is also, though, a context in which other answers are being offered by better-budgeted competitors, skilled in the arts of bedazzlement, who elbow their way in and get a hearing (which is frustrating). In our privileged position of having people come to us with the most profound and intimate of needs we are jostled by fast-talking and big-promising others. We are not the only preachers on the block. If we cannot make good on what people want done for them spiritually, there are plenty around who will—or say they will.

A cursory sorting out of people's expectations (at least the kind that get channeled through the conduit of the pastoral vocation) ends up with two piles, miracles and answers. The miracles are an expectation that God will do for us what we cannot do for ourselves; the answers are an expectation that God will tell us what we can't figure out for ourselves. Both expectations are plausible, having a certain commonsense reality to them. Since God is both omnipotent and omniscient it would seem to follow that if we get close to him some of what he is ought to rub off on us. It is not unreasonable to suppose that his power will rub off in the form of miracles and his wisdom in the form of answers.

When pastors look around at what their competitors are offering, most of it is classifiable, also, in terms of miracles and answers. In a supply-demand marketplace there is, I suppose, a certain inevitability in this correlation between what is wanted and what is offered. At this point pastoral work encounters a complex difficulty, for the vocation of pastor does not permit trafficking in either miracles or answers. Pastors are in the awkward position of refusing to give what a great many people assume it is our assigned job to give. We are in the embarassing position of disappointing people in what they think they have a perfect right to get from us. We are asked to pray for an appropriate miracle; we are called upon to declare an authoritative answer. But our calling equips us for neither. In fact, it forbids us to engage in either the miracle business or the answer business.

"Vanity of Vanities!"

Caught in this crossfire of religious expectations, the pastor finds the book of Ecclesiastes* a most welcome ally, for it represents a pastoral position worked out *vis a vis* miracle-mongers and answer-makers. It does not direct pastors in what to do, but it is of immense help in telling us what we need not do, in fact, *must* not do. There is no program for pastoral work in the document, but its brilliantly articulated rejection of what it is dangerous to do makes it indispensable.

Qoheleth's pastoral evaluation of the state of religion in his time is summed up in the word *hebel.* It "connotes what is visible or recognizable, but unsubstantial, momentary, and profitless."[2] Various meanings glance off the surface of the word as the context shifts; futility, spuriousness, illusion, fraud. Qoheleth uses the word forty times, both beginning (1:2) and ending (12:8) with it (in the rest of the OT it is used but thirty-three times). Often he uses it in an emphatic form, *hebel hebelim,* "vanity of vanities!" (or, as Frank Zimmerman irreverantly translates, "flatulence!").[3]

"It is evident," wrote Karl Barth, "that, just as genuine coins are open to suspicion so long as false coins are in circulation, so the

---

*In this section Ecclesiastes will be used to refer to the book, and Qoheleth will designate the author.

perception which proceeds outwards from God cannot have free course until the arrogance of religion be done away."[4] That announces Qoheleth's program: he will drive out from Israel and church all who trade with fraudulent coin, and sweep the place clean with his broom, *hebel.*

The precise historical setting in which Qoheleth wrote is not known. The general period in which he is known to have lived— late Persian and early Greek (ca. 350 to 250 B.C.)—is one of the least known periods in biblical history. The writer is a question mark and the times in which he wrote a haze. In that situation nothing can be set down as certain. But nothing is spoken or written in a vacuum; Qoheleth did write in a particular environment consisting of real people dealing with actual ideas. And so in the absence of hard historical data it is not out of place, I think, to conjecture a religious situation that fits what is known of Qoheleth's century, namely, that it was a peacetime culture of moderate prosperity in which religion, unaggravated by serious conflict, goes to seed. Relaxed after the vigorous energy output of early growth, and released from the tensions of conflict, one senses a kind of slackness. John Bright notes that in the post-exilic centuries there was a general "loosening of religion from the context of history."[5]

Under such conditions two things developed which, if unchecked, would have been (and nearly were) the death of healthy, biblical faith: overconfident wisdom and nervous apocalyptic. There is a certain typicality to both of these excesses. They are recurrent throughout the story of faith: overconfident piety, sure that it knows God's mind better than he does himself, and neurotic apocalyptic, sure that doomsday is just around the corner. Since both positions use a biblical vocabulary and have religious goals, pastors are expected to be on hand to assist in their implementation.

Ecclesiastes was among the last books of the Old Testament to be written. Given the way things were going in Judaism at the time, it is not a natural or obvious conclusion to what we know of the trends. We could very well have had something quite different: for instance, a smart-aleck composition by a committee of solomonic epigoni (from the late-wisdom movement) or, perhaps, a lurid end-of-the-world chart, with illustrations drawn from the visions of

Ezekiel and Daniel. We have neither. We have, instead, the sardonic lines of Qoheleth, who refused the easy complacency of the humanists and rejected the phobic obsessions of the apocalypticists. He refused to cater to the demands for either warmed-over wisdom or half-baked apocalyptic for which there was, and continues to be, such a ready market.

Qoheleth seems to have been faced with what both St. Paul and St. John encountered in the early church, described by Hoskyns and Davey as "a riot of disordered religious romanticism . . . confidently declared to be the essence of the Christian faith." In dealing with it each apostle "put forth his whole pastoral and literary energy in order to recover the control of the Church by the Life and Death of Jesus".[6]

Ecclesiastes is a John the Baptist kind of book. It functions not as a meal but as a bath. It is not nourishment; it is cleansing. It is repentance. It is purging. The pastor reads Ecclesiastes to get scrubbed clean from illusion and sentiment, from ideas that are idolatrous and feelings that cloy. It is an exposé and rejection of every pretentious and presumptious expectation aimed at God and routed through the pastor. Walther Eichrodt, always masterly in his summaries, wrote:

> Against the self-confident wisdom teaching, which took on a new lease of life in the Hellenistic period as a result of an acquaintance with Greek philosophy, and presumed to initiate men into God's counsels and to resolve the enigmas of the world, there came out to battle a man intimately acquainted with the thought of the wise, and himself a member of their circle (12:9). In constantly fresh turns of thought he made his sallies against the claim of wisdom to supremacy, in order to destroy its false prestige, and to confront it with the fact that One higher than the wise had appointed bounds that it was not to pass.[7]

"I, the Qoheleth"

One insight into the pastoral importance of this work is provided by a grammatical observation: the author designates himself "I the Preacher," (1:12) "preacher" being the English translation of the Hebrew *Qoheleth* and the Greek *Ecclesiastes.* The word is based on a verb *(qhl)* which means "to gather together, to assemble." Grammatically the form, a feminine participle, turns the verb into an occupational designation. (There are other instances in Ezra 2:55, *tsophereth*, and in Ezra 2:57, *pokhereth*.) The Qoheleth, then, is " 'an assembler of people into the presence of God' "[8]—a function which is carried out today by Christian pastors. Since the word is clearly not a personal name but a reference to an office, the contents of the book very likely have to do with concerns that a religious leader in the community has for the health of the people who assemble under his or her leadership.

One of the characteristics of pastoral work, for some the most pervasive thrust, is the development of mature, personal relationships with a personal God, the translation of the bloodless abstractions of theology into personal instances of discipleship. The pervasive danger in the work is that while developing and encouraging personal relationships with God, the difference between God and humanity is denied and the distance between holiness and sinfulness is obscured. Relationship with God is banalized into a chummy acquaintance with The Man Upstairs.

In all Hebrew and Christian experience there is a strong sense of the permanent gulf between God and humanity.

> This predominant trait in the personal relationship of Man with God in the Old Testament is given linguistic expression in the habit of describing the whole religious relationship as *the fear of God* or *of Yahweh*, *yir'at 'elōhīm* or *yir'at yhwh*, and likewise, right religious conduct is termed God- or Yahweh-fearing, *yᵉrē ᵉlōhīm (yhwh)*, a usage which persists with remarkable regularity from the earliest to the latest times.[9]

"The end of the matter; all has been heard. Fear God, and keep his commandments; for this is the whole duty of man." (12:13)

The view of some, that Qoheleth was a quirky eccentric far out of the mainstream of Judaism, working on a private death-of-god theology (Johannes Hemple describes his work as " 'the most heretical book of the third century B.C.' ")[10] is unlikely. Without evidence to the contrary (and there isn't any) the fact that the author is referred to by his occupational title, combined with the fact that his occupation was public, produces the natural assumption that he did his work somewhere near the center of the stream of Judaism. Thus

Robert Gordis, the best Jewish commentator on the book, concludes, "It is clear that our book is in the mainstream of Jewish literature, drawing upon the past and contributing to the future."[11] The problem Qoheleth faced was that the center of the stream was clogged with religious debris and theological junk. The river of God's revelation was no longer flowing freely—it was backing up from a log jam of staggering proportions. The white-water faith of early Israel, clean and rapid in its flow, was now collecting in pools in the clogged-up stream bed. And the waters were starting to stink from stagnation. Worse, enterprising entrepreneurs had set up shop on the banks and were bottling the polluted stuff and selling it as holy water to the tourists. Qoheleth would have none of it. He protested. He debunked. He assembled the people and told them that the holy water was a fraud and if they drank it they would get dysentery. His, undeniably, was a minority voice, but it was a voice spoken from the center of the stream. He remains a faithful guardian of that divine otherness which cannot be absorbed into any human system. "God has made it so, in order that men should fear before him." (3:14)

"I Commend Enjoyment"

Ecclesiastes is sometimes dismissed with the labels "cynical" and "pessimistic." But the labels won't stick. There is too much evidence of robust cheerfulness. "I commend enjoyment" (8:15) is a theme recurrent throughout (2:24; 3:13; 8:15; 9:7–10; 11:7). In the Jerusalem Talmud *(Kiddushin)* there is a saying, "Every man must render an account before God of all the good things he beheld in life and did not enjoy,"[12] a saying very much in the spirit of Ecclesiastes.

The center of the stream of biblical literature can be characterized by God's yes. That word expresses, perhaps better than any other, the gospel message. God says yes to humanity. Humanity returns the yes. Pastoral work consists in repeating the gospel yes in every conceivable life situation and encouraging the yes answer of faith. St. Paul's text is programmatic for the pastoral task: "For the Son of God, Jesus Christ, whom we preached among you . . . was not Yes and No; but in him it is always Yes. For all the promises of

Yes

God find their Yes in him. That is why we utter the Amen through him to the glory of God." (2 Cor. 1:19-20) *Yes* in Hebrew is *Amen.* It is rich and allusive in meaning. It indicates firmness, solidity. It describes what is nailed down. God is Amen (Isa. 65:16)—sure, faithful, affirmative. Because God is Amen people can live in Amen, that is, in faith. We are taught to say yes to the God who says yes to us in Christ and so be connected in an affirmative way with the God who has redeemed us.

This is the stream in which Qoheleth worked, the same stream in which every pastor works still. But in Qoheleth's times the stream was not moving and the waters were not clear. The affirmations of God had been torn from their rooted context along the banks of the river of God. Instead of growing and bearing fruit they were so much dead wood, blocking the flow of worship and muddying the refracted clarities of truth. God's yes was being spoken and used apart from God himself. That is no uncommon experience in either Israel or church. There is an incredible amount of sheer bilge that tries to pass itself off for religion. So it is not enough that a pastor repeat the yes—it must be a rooted yes, a yes that is organically alive in the biblical interchanges between an affirming God and a responding person.

For the kerygmatic yes is not the equivilant of saying "everything is ok—everything will turn out all right." The pastor is not Micawber, smiling his way through the apocalypse, assuring wife, children, and friends that "something will turn up." The yes of the gospel is not spoken under the pretense that sin is not as bad as it appears to be, nor while avoiding pain, nor while sidestepping suffering. The yes spoken in the course of pastoral work is ruinously emptied of meaning if it settles for semi-sanctified boosterism. The pastor is not a cheerleader. Pastoral enthusiasm used for propagandistic ends blunts the fine edge of the divine yes. Pastors have little to learn and much to fear from the public relations industry.

Amen, the biblical yes, is used, always, in relation to God, the God who establishes and makes persons firm and secure in eternal purpose and redemptive love. In response to that affirmation we say Amen—Yes. It is God's most characteristic word; it is humankind's most appropriate response. Scriptural citations show that the affirmation is both comprehensive and detailed.

Persons say Amen when they want to confirm the acceptance of a task assigned to them by God. When David directed his court prophet and priest to set apart Solomon to the kingship and gave directions on how to do it, one of the men shouted Amen (1 Kings 1:36); that is, "we understand our instructions; we believe that this is the will of God; we will do it!"

Amen is used as a response of the individual to something inward and private with God—a personal yes to God. When Jeremiah was asked by God to be the prophet of reform in the years of Josiah, he gave a single word of response, Amen (Jer. 11:5); "Yes, Lord, I will be the person you want me to be in these difficult days."

Amen corroborates prayer and praise when it is used to give individual attestation to public litanies and hymns in worship. When David brought the ark up to Jerusalem and organized the services of worship, the choir sang a song of praise in which all that the people felt in joy to God was assembled in exhaustive detail. The concluding word was a great, unison Amen (1 Chron. 16:36): "Yes, that is exactly what we want to say and sing."

It was a favorite word with Jesus. He prefaced many of his sayings with the word Amen, often with the double Amen (verily, verily, or truly, truly). The point was to show not only that his sayings were reliable and true, but that they were so because Jesus himself in his Amen made response to them, validating and "faithing" them. He joined the yes of God and the yes of humankind over the total range of human experience.

The usage has been persistent and the emphasis extraordinary in both Israel and church. It is the most powerful word we have for both proclamation and response. It gathers to itself an entire history of "yea-saying," making the blessings of God operative in the community and thus characterizing Christian ministry. As the pastor centers and affirms the yes, he or she participates in biblical ministry as one "who accepts [God's] word as true and certain . . . one who acknowledges and affirms it in his own life and thus causes it, as fulfilled by him, to become a demand to others."[13]

The preaching event in Israel that collected the divine yes into a comprehensive act of worship was the Feast of Tabernacles. The kerygmatic theme of Tabernacles worship was God's bounty and blessing. It combined the seasonal festivities of a harvest festival (bounty) with the historical memories of miraculous preservation in the wilderness (blessing).[14] It was a time of plenty and rejoicing. The natural goodness of creation (the grain harvest) and the supernatural goodness of providence (the miracle bread, manna) represented the preached truth that God gives abundant life to his people; "my cup runneth over . . ." "All the promises of God find their Yes in him." (2 Cor. 1:20) The theme continues to be repeated every time Christians gather for worship, offering gifts and lifting praise. Most significantly, Ecclesiastes was assigned reading for Tabernacles. The most negative of the scrolls was required reading at the most positive of the festivals. The joining together of Tabernacles and Ecclesiastes is plainly pastoral, for as long as people are in touch, via common worship, with the God of blessing, the yes maintains its character as God's yes. But if at any point there is a separation between the God of blessing and the blessings of God, between the God of providence and his miraculous provisions, grave dangers threaten the life of the people of God at the point of the separation.[15]

To one who is unacquainted with the holy history out of which God's blessing is articulated, or to one who fails to participate in the pilgrim worship in which God's bounty is remembered, blessing can easily be supposed to be no more than a commodity available for purchase or trade. Pastors deal with such suppositions daily. They know how easily and frequently a sentimental deity is drawn with the chalk of pious illusions—a wish-fulfillment god—and identified, presumptuously, with the God who blesses. A religion that promises the fulfillment of all *needs* is thus distorted into a religion that manipulates God for the satisfaction of all *wants*. When that happens the pastor has to say no. Pastors have a supernatural gospel to affirm and a divine yes to repeat to a people who naively suppose that any kind of talk that has a tone of spiritual uplift to it is a gospel, and who uncritically accept as a guide anyone who cheerily tells them that they will get better. The fact is that everything that is done and spoken in the name of God is not good. Everything that happens does not turn out all right if only we put a happy face on it. Jesus warned his disciples shortly before he parted from them: " 'And then if any one says to you, "Look, here is the Christ!" or "Look, there he is!" Do not believe it. False Christs and false prophets will arise and show signs and wonders to lead astray, if possible, the elect. But take heed; I have told you all things beforehand.'" (Mark 13:21–23)

Whenever the warm blessings of Tabernacles are celebrated the cool wisdom of Ecclesiastes needs to be remembered. In the world of religion, Ecclesiastes is an indispensable, even if unpopular, pastoral voice. For the pastor has the responsibility to nurture the affirmative without encouraging the gullible; to keep people alert and prepared to say yes to every yes of God in every part of existence without at the same time being a patsy for every confidence game in town; to train people in robust acceptance of what God brings to us and not to passively submit to the trashy merchandising of religious salespeople. We must confront the breezy, irresponsible nonchalance that avoids hard difficulties and shuts its eyes to the worst suffering. We must demonstrate that the trumpet sentence "in him it is always Yes" can only be sounded in a world in which Job's doubt and pain is affirmed, a world in which David's disentegrating family and harassed kingship is accepted, a world in which Peter's denials and bitter weeping are acknowledged—a world of shipwreck and rejection, famine and plague, a world in which Jesus Christ hangs on a cross feeling in every nerve-end the physical and spiritual disorder of a world which says no to God.

Qoheleth serves this pastoral function by challenging the naive optimism which assumes that being on God's side carries with it the comfortable wisdom that solves all difficulties, and by countering the gushing expectation of convenient miracles. His detached skepticism is a pastoral negation to unbiblical expectations of what God does and will do, expectations that project upon God what we want him to do for us and interfere with our being open to what he has already revealed that he will do for us in Christ. He exposes the religion of the ghost-written bestseller and the television spectacular, and prepares, via repentance, for faith-response to the gospel.

Qoheleth on his own and by himself does not say all this. But in the context in which we have him, set, that is, in the wide biblical stream of affirmation (the canon) he does. Hertzberg, in his commentary,[16] has very finely demonstrated, in detail, that Qoheleth has modeled his view of life on the creation story in Genesis, which is one of the most forceful affirmations ever written. He knows that the Creator has made everything beautiful in its time and has put eternity in the human's heart, thus binding the human species inwardly to himself. This, too, is why joy can be praised as the first of the Creator's gifts (2:24; 3:1–8, 22; 8:15; 9:7; 11:9), wisdom can be recognized as a high good within its limits (2:13f., 26; 4:13; 7:4f.; 9:16ff.) and people can be encouraged to faithful labor (9:10; 11:6). All Qoheleth's pastoral negations are set in the context of God's affirmations. God is the living center of everything we are and everything we do. He is before, behind, over, beneath everything. If we separate any part of our lives from him, we are left holding an empty bag. Nothing can stand on its own as a good, apart from God. Anything wrenched from its context in God's creation and God's salvation is without substance. It is either God or nothing (hebel). No idea, no feeling, no truth, no pleasure can exist on its own.

For as long as persons try to make a religion without God and achieve wholeness without faith, Qoheleth's ministry must be repeated. He is the primary biblical voice that insists that religion taken out of context is vanity; he will admit no pleasure, possession, or piety to an independent existence. He strips us of "religion" so that we might be dressed for God.

"Besides Being Wise"

An appreciation of Qoheleth's pastoral significance is heightened by locating him in Israel's leadership traditions. Israel's leadership flowed, basically, through three channels—priestly, prophetic, and wisdom (" '. . . for the law shall not perish from the priest, nor counsel from the wise, nor the word from the prophet' " Jer. 18:18).

Priests presided over a system of worship that exhibited all the relationships between persons and God. Their traditions were collected in the first division of the Hebrew canon, the Law (torah). Their rituals demonstrated a process of confession and forgiveness, of petition and promise, that kept the people in touch with the experiences of the Exodus and the words from Sinai. All the great acts and words of God were kept before the hearts of the people and made available for the responses of faith.

Prophets spoke the word of God to the people. Their traditions were collected in the second great division of the Hebrew canon. In every generation there was a fresh, contemporary expression of the will of God, the age-old word of God articulated in the language and idiom of the present.

The wise men were learned men in the community who taught and trained the people to use what they knew of God's way in everyday routines. The results of their work are in a final grouping in the canon, the Writings. They took as their specialty the everyday world of work and sex, pleasure and leisure, family and community relationships, how you treat a son, a wife, a slave, a neighbor. Ecclesiastes is the final book in this tradition to be included in the Hebrew canon. (In the Greek Bible, Sirach-Ecclesiasticus, written a hundred years later, was also included).

Wisdom had its concrete setting in the daily lives of a people who believed in God as Savior and Creator.[17] That is, the wise men worked in a context previously established and defined by priests and prophets. What they did in that context was not so much announce the word of God, as train people in the skills of living it. In that way they functioned very much as Christian pastors today in their work between Sundays. They used the gathered experience and insights of the wisdom traditions in education of the young and in practical living among a people whom God had redeemed.

Sometimes, though, this wisdom got dislodged from its priestly-prophetic context and tried to function as a thing on its own. When that happened, protests were filed. The most famous of these protests are Job and Ecclesiastes. But they aren't the only ones. Isaiah, for instance published the oracle:

> "Because this people draw near with their mouth
>   and honor me with their lips,
>   while their hearts are far from me,
> and their fear of me is a commandment of men learned by rote;
> therefore, behold, I will again
>   do marvelous things with this people,
>   wonderful and marvelous;

and the wisdom of their wise men shall perish,
and the discernment of their discerning men shall be hid."
(Isa. 29:13–14)

The wise men according to Isaiah were repeating old saws and mumbling old formulas, saying things that had a sound of orthodoxy but with no personal involvement or spiritual commitment to them. (See also Isaiah 31:1–3; 30:1–7; 19:11–15.) A hundred years later, Jeremiah was up against the same things and spoke his protest against the arrogant self-confidence of the sages:

> Thus says the LORD: . . . "let not the mighty man glory in his might, let not the rich man glory in his riches; but let him who glories glory in this, that he understands and knows me, that I am the LORD who practice steadfast love, justice, and righteousness in the earth; for in these things I delight, says the LORD." (Jer. 9:23–24)

Whatever else wisdom does, it does not qualify a person to function on his or her own, apart from God.

These citations from Isaiah and Jeremiah are peripheral evidence that wisdom did not always work within the liturgical-kerygmatic framework, as had been intended; the major evidence, though is in the books of Job and Ecclesiastes. Proverbs (from the early period) and Sirach (from the late period) show wisdom functioning in its healthy state in Israelite history. In between, Job and Ecclesiastes are protests against wisdom's decadence.

Job rages against wisdom that has lost touch with the living realities of God during a time of suffering. The book originated, probably, in the early years of Babylonian exile to protest the shallow theodicies of the wisdom teachers. The wise men had professed to be able to instruct people in a way of life that would guarantee that they would be "healthy, wealthy, and wise." The Babylonian destruction of Jerusalem and ensuing exile, besides being an obvious judgment on a nation that had rejected God's love and spurned a life of faith, also touched good and innocent people who were hurt, killed, and deported. There must have been many who had participated honestly and enthusiastically in the Josianic reform, who had responded to the deuteronomic preaching and lived ardently and faithfully in righteousness. According to the propaganda of the wise men they should have been exempt from suffering. But they weren't. They suffered along with everyone else.

And so, Job, on behalf of these people who had been misled by the platitudes of the wisdom teachers, issued this anguished rejoinder. He rejected the kind of advice and teaching that has God all figured out and provides glib explanations for every exception. The writer drew the guileless, innocent Job against a background of immense suffering, and then assembled all the wise man's counsel around him (in the form of speeches by Eliphaz, Bildad, Zophar, and Elihu). The contrast is unforgettable: the counselors, methodically and pedantically reciting their bookish precepts, over against Job, first raging in pain and roaring blasphemies, and then silent in awe-struck faith before God who speaks "out of the whirlwind." There are times when wise men must simply shut up and let God speak.

The book of Job does not reject wisdom. It is, in fact, written from within the wisdom movement. What it rejects is wisdom reduced to bromides and wisdom merchandized in success stories.

By the fourth century the task needed doing again. Wisdom had again grown stale and become commonplace. But the historical setting was now very different. The problem now was not bewilderment caused by suffering but complacencies induced by prosperity. Qoheleth, with a wholly different style, did for his generation what Job had done for his. Whereas Job used dramatic forms, drawing on colorful, mythic metaphors, Qoheleth used subtlety and wit, the prose of "fine hammered steel" so much admired by Herman Melville.[18] (Melville's admiration of Qoheleth is somewhat surprising, and therefore all the more interesting, for Melville himself functioned more in the manner of Job by introducing the curses of Captain Ahab and the thrashings of Moby Dick into the quiet Emersonian gardens of nineteeth century transcendentalism).[19] In the late fourth century the faith of Israel had become flat and platitudinous. The majestic mountain of revelation, Sinai, had been eroded into a dull hillock. The thundering commands of God (Psalm 29) had been muted and recomposed into soothing background music. The soul-stirring encounters between a sinful man and a holy God had been sentimentalized into soap opera melodrama. The tremendous austerities of the desert where a homeless people had found themselves, miraculously, guided and provisioned by a God of mercy and love, had been surveyed, marked out in quarter-acre lots, and put on sale at a price every middle-class family could afford. And now, instead of the penetrating, foundation-shaking wisdom of a Moses they had the cliches of positive thinkers; instead of the "artful thunder" of Isaiah they had the oily showmanship of television hucksters.

There was plenty of wisdom around, but it was wisdom in the wrong place—bits and pieces of God's revelation, taken out of their original and awesome settings and arranged like bric-a-brac (easy answers and convenient miracles) in the culture. Brilliant, cadenced poetry and thunderous prose had been condensed into *Reader's Digest* reprints, ready to be handed out for conversation pieces. The environment was cluttered with the artifacts of religious small talk. It was the kind of thing that Saul Bellow's Augie March objected to in his mother: "It was kitchen religion and had nothing to do with the giant God of the Creation who turned back the waters and exploded Gomorrah, but it was on the side of religion."[20]

How refreshing—and how important—to have the modest wisdom of Ecclesiastes introduced into this scene. For Ecclesiastes is wisdom that "knows its place." "Besides being wise" (12:9) Qoheleth went about his work as teacher and scribe, sure of the importance of his work but sure also of its limitations.

"Eternity into Man's Mind"

There are, of course, *answers* in biblical religion. The Christian faith deals in matters of revelation; we learn the character of God and the nature of his will. Guesswork and mystification are abolished in the light of the revelation of Jesus Christ. There is *content* to biblical religion, content which can be examined historically and tested philosophically. There is more than "hints followed by guesses." Some of the knowledge of God can be formulated into sentences that are answers to questions people ask.

So it is not answers, as such, which are being rejected. A wholesale rejection of answers would end up with a religion of dark rooms, incense, and mumbo jumbo. Qoheleth's polemic is directed against the *secularization* of answers—taking knowledge which has its source in God, detaching it from the source, and then using it *ad hoc.*

Religious discourse that is removed from its kerygmatic-liturgical origins very quickly becomes the merest sophistry, truth *about* God divorced from the mind *of* God.

> For in much wisdom is much vexation,
> and he who increases knowledge increases sorrow.
>
> (1:18)

Walter Harrelson concludes that this is what is most useful and most characteristic in Ecclesiastes: "A crashing destruction of idols, of easy answers to the question of life's meaning—including religious answers—sounds throughout this book."[21]

The people who pose religious questions are sincere enough. But they are also, very often, only peripherally interested in God. Information about God? Yes. Useful insights derivative from God? Yes. But God? No. They sidestep the biblical knowledge that always involves intimacy and commitment. They maintain a conveniently safe distance between themselves and the commands of God. But they ask questions.

Every generation has religious leaders who cater to the demand and give answers. Three hundred years after the time of Qoheleth it was the Pharisees. They had a solution for every problem, an example for every situation, an answer for every question. One day one of them made the mistake of engaging Jesus in what he surely intended to be no more than a street-corner discussion: "What is the best answer of all?"

> "Which commandment is the first of all?" Jesus answered, . . . " 'The Lord our God, the Lord is one; and you shall love the Lord your God with all your heart, and with all your soul, and with all your mind, and with all your strength." The second is this, 'You shall love your neighbor as yourself.' " (Mark 12:28–31)

Jesus' answer is as instructive as it is interesting to persons who have religious questions posed to them. He first anchors his statement *about* God in a relationship *with* God: " 'The Lord our God, the Lord is one.' " The sentence is an ancient confession of faith from Deuteronomy (6:4). He then formulates a double command in which all that is known and understood about God is directed into an act of love: for God and the neighbor. The cognitive aspect of knowledge is not minimized; but it is stated in such a way that it can only be used in faith and discipleship.

Jesus' answer is exemplary for pastors and all others who are asked to provide knowledge of God in the form of answers to questions. The only way to keep knowledge from becoming separated from relationship with God is to return to the confessional base of worship—the preaching and worship of Deuteronomy. Knowledge of God comes from scriptures proclaimed and obeyed in the community of the people of God. At no time do we have biblical information or theological knowledge which comes down to us apart from the context. Everything we know about God comes out of the preaching and praying communities of Israel and church. Truths about God are not found, like arrowheads in old fields, by people off by themselves hunting souvenirs.

When religious knowledge becomes an impersonal item of information, or is used impersonally, it ceases to be biblical. If it is used to put distance between persons, something has gone wrong. If it is used to put another person in his or her "place" something has gone wrong. If it is used to improve life apart from faith in God, something has gone wrong. And if the pastor collaborates in any of these transactions, he or she is an accessory to the sin.

Reading between the lines of Qoheleth, it is apparent that the wise men of the time were isolated from the large context in which God created, provided, and redeemed. They had taken bits of insight and smatterings of wisdom acquired through the years and put them to use in making people successful and happy. They were no longer in correspondence with prophets attuned to the powerful, life-changing word of God. They had lost touch with priests living with the agonies and sufferings of guilty and oppressed people. They were, in fact, dilletantes—intellectual dandies who cheerily passed on their proverbs of success and threw out snippets of advice. They were as up to date as Ann Landers and as impersonal as the horoscope. One of our own poets, similar in many ways to Qoheleth, addressed the equivalent situation in our century with the line, "Knowledge of words, and ignorance of the WORD."[22]

Qoheleth's typical and pungent insight is in the enigmatic phrase, "he has put eternity into man's mind, yet so that he cannot find out what God has done from the beginning to the end." (3:11) The mind is in touch with eternity and restless to know the mysteries of God's being; the mind so affected can never be satisfied with mere answers but only with God himself who is more than answers.

"You Do Not Know the Work of God"

And there are, of course, *miracles* in biblical religion. The Christian faith deals in matters of salvation. We worship a God who does things for us that we cannot do for ourselves. God is not the sum total of what humanity is in the process of learning about itself, and the world around it, and the universe. God is the Other. Miracles are evidence that there are dimensions to God that with all our knowledge we have not been able to anticipate. To believe in a miracle is only a way of saying that God is free—free to do a new thing. He is not bound to a deterministic creation of natural cause and effect. He is not trapped in his own cosmic machine. He is free above and beyond what we observe of his ways. He is free to do whatever he wills, whether it conforms to what we have observed as the laws he established in creation, or not, whether they are part of the routine expectations we have come to associate with the nature he created in us, or not.

Miracle is the usual word for describing items that are a surprise to us, events that are outside our expectations and beyond our abilities. Miracle is the word we use to describe that which is beyond what we thought would happen in the world as created, or other than what we had supposed God would do.

A religion without miracles has only marginal worth; why bother with religion if you can do it all yourself anyway? But a religion with miracles is in constant peril of being misunderstood as privileged access to the supernatural.

The pastor has the difficult task of encouraging faith in the God who works miracles—heals the sick, delivers the oppressed, saves the lost—and at the same time warning against believing in miracles as such; that is, the supernatural separated from personal relationships with God and his people. For the supernatural is not always the divine. "How many silly miracles there are/That will not save us."[23] Jeremiah rebuked false prophets: his oracle posts a notice often seen in the corridors of biblical religion, "The prophets prophesy lies in my name; I sent them not . . . they prophesy unto you a lying vision and divination, and a thing of nought, and the deceit of their own heart." (Jer. 14:14, author's translation) The early church found it necessary also to warn of the spurious but without smothering vitality. In his earliest writings Paul holds the two elements in balance: "Do not quench the Spirit, do not despise prophesying, but test everything." (1 Thess. 5:19–21)[24]

The gospel message says: "You don't live in a mechanistic world ruled by necessity; you don't live in a random world ruled by chance; you live in a world ruled by the God of Exodus and Easter. He will do things in you that neither you nor your friends would have supposed possible. He is not limited by anything you think you know about him; he is not boxed into the cramped dimensions of your ignorance or your despair. As Isaiah says, 'Behold, I am doing a new thing.' " (Isa. 43:19) But pastoral difficulties develop when people, on hearing that kind of exhortation, instead of putting trust in the God who is able to work beyond our expectations, attempt to find a point of leverage at which they can pry a miracle out of God to satisfy what they think they need. Miracle for them has almost nothing to do with God; it is a demand item which will get them what they want.

In such a way religion is misunderstood as a kind of technology of the supernatural: it provides the know-how to get things done when physicians give up, when counselors fail, when the economy disintegrates. If one learns to pray according to the correct formulas and has "enough faith" a miracle can be produced.

But that is not what the Bible, ever, means by miracle. True, miracles are evidence of a God who does things we cannot do for ourselves. But it is not a power that is put at our disposal. The function of miracles, biblically, is to break open reality so that we see existence in its essence, see beneath the surface routines we took as the whole picture, and we have revealed to us what was hidden by our stubborn insistence on sense-data or our slow-witted faith, and have more and more of our lives drawn into the healing-saving orbit of personal love. Chesterton drew attention "to the fact that Christ worked his miracles not to escape time but to plunge men into the choices time presses upon them."[25]

Qoheleth lived in a culture that was just beginning to develop an exaggerated appetite for miracle, and warned them: "As you do not know how the spirit comes to the bones in the womb of a woman with child, so you do not know the work of God who makes everything." (11:5) The same conditions that produced a secularization of answers produced in the succeeding generations a secularization of miracles. A hundred years after Qoheleth we know that Judaism was inundated with books about the supernatural quite apart from any trust in God. The complex angelologies and demonologies, and the endless speculations about heaven and hell that fill the books of 2 Esdras, 2 Enoch, Jubilees, and the Testament of the Twelve Patriarchs are the result of what was already incipient in Qoheleth's century.

Israel, unequivocally committed to a God who did wonders and performed miracles, also had a long tradition of saying no to any and all secularization of miracle. The proper relationship of humanity to God (humble trust, obedient adoration) was preserved by the exclusion from their worship of all magical practices by means of which a human might be able to exert pressure on the deity.[26] Even though nothing in Ecclesiastes refers specifically to the purveyors of miracles (the sorcerers, diviners, and necromancers) the acerbic rejection of all religious tomfoolery effectively excludes them in a proleptic way.

It takes no great act of imagination to hear Qoheleth's intonations in these sentences written by Diogenes Allen:

> For many, religion—both bizarre and the ordinary Christian variety —is a means to success in business, gaining or preserving health, protection against harm, and attaining a never-ending existence. The theory that God functions as a crutch for man, who cannot stand on his own two feet, does not begin to convey the brashness of the phenomenon. Plugging into the supernatural is more like a greedy exploitation of a bonanza.
>
> I used to think that my task as a philosopher and a clergyman was to keep the possibility of God at least open—as though the struggle were between religion or no religion. I now have become aware that a more pressing problem is not a shortage of religion, but far too much *bad* religion. Put more precisely, the problem is that once one lets the "supernatural" in at all, how does one draw the line between

what is permissible and what is not? If, for example, one accepts miracles, demons, angels, and telepathy, then why not astrology, fortune-telling, premonitions of the future, ghosts, witches, werewolves, and vampires?[27]

There is a vast literature and an extensive cultus that supposes that the power of God can be bought by reading the right book, by imitating the most impressive leader, by discovering the workable formula. This power can then be put to the use of growing churches, expanding membership, filling people with the Holy Spirit, taking off weight, running stewardship campaigns, exorcising demons, curing cancer, getting rid of communists, *ad infinitum, ad absurdum.*

St. Peter's encounter with Simon the Magician is a good pastoral case-study in this area. Simon was genuinely attracted to the gospel. There is no question of insincerity in the story as Luke tells it in Acts, chapter 8. Simon saw the gospel as a superior version of what he had himself been engaged in as a magician—a way of getting things done, a manipulation of the supernatural for personal purposes (often trivial and sometimes base), and then commercialized into the art of saying or doing things that entertain, impress, or amaze the uninitiated.

Magic and faith have one thing in common: they both deal with the supernatural. But everything else is different, for magic is an impersonal manipulation and control, a way of *getting,* while faith is a personal response to God, inviting him to do what he will in us, an *offering* of obedience to walk where he leads. We come to God not to get our way but to get his; not to acquire a means of impressing our friends with our access to power but to let him make an eternal impression on us with his salvation. The greed for miracles is expressed in Simon's request: " 'Give me also this power. . . .' " (Acts 8:19) The hunger for God is expressed in Benjamin Schmolcks' hymn: "My Jesus, as Thou wilt! O may Thy will be mine! Into Thy hand of love I would my all resign. Through sorrow or through joy, Conduct me as Thine own; And help me still to say, 'My Lord, Thy will be done.' "

Religious leaders (pastors!) perpetuate Simon's sin when they encourage people to come to God in order to get "power." All who preach formulas, who promise rewards, who nurture the supposition that gain, whether financial, physical, or emotional, can be gotten out of the gospel, fall under the ban: " 'Your silver perish with you!' " (Acts 8:20)

"Be Not Righteous Overmuch"

The conflict between Baalism and Yahwism in Canaan provides one of the most useful orientations for pastors who must give spiritual counsel and lead in common worship among people who are religious but are not yet, or not maturely, Christian.[28] The centuries-long episode is an extended illustration of Qoheleth's admonition: "Be not righteous overmuch, and do not make yourself overwise; why should you destroy yourself?" (7·16) Pastors who feel this history in their bones, a history involving decades of stormy competition between the cult of Baal and the community of Yahweh, will have absorbed the kind of theological and liturgical insights that develop a sure hand in conserving the authentic core of biblical experience while leading Christians to pray and worship intelligently and responsibly.

Baalism was the worship of the Canaanites when Israel occupied the land under Joshua. It continued as a competitive threat to the worship of Israel until the time of the Exile. Sometimes it was terminated, other times suppressed. Sometimes it broke out and dominated the entire culture.

The emphasis of Baalism was on psychophysical relatedness and subjective experience. The gulf between people and God was leveled out of existence by means of participatory rites. The terrifying majesty of God, his "otherness," was assimilated to the religious passions of the worshiper. The god of the bull image, the god of wine, the god of the fertility figurine was the god of relevance, fulfilling personal needs with convincing immediacy. The desires that inflamed the soul were fulfilled in the cultic act of worship. The transcendence of the deity was overcome in the ecstasy of feeling.

Sensory participation was featured. Images were necessary—the bolder, the more colorful, the more sensational, the better. Music and dance became the means for drawing persons out of their private diversities and merging them into a mass response. Sexual activity in the cult was frequent since it achieved the primary Baalistic goal so completely—the ecstatic plunge of the whole sensory person into the passion of the religious moment.

Sacred prostitution thus became the supreme expression of Baalism. It was rooted in magical, homeopathic practices designed to ensure increased fertility and secure divine power through sexual intimacy. Prostitutes, male and female, (the *qadesh* and *q'desha* of Canaan) were standard accompaniments of the worship of Baal (or Asherah).

When, for instance, Ahab imported the Melkart cult, Jehu summed it up as simply whoredom and witchcraft (2 Kings 9:22). "Harlotry" was the stock criticism of the worship of the people when it had been assimilated to Baalistic forms (Hos. 1ff.; Jer. 3:1ff.; Ezek. 16 and 23; Amos 2:7; Hos. 4:13; Jer. 5:7; 13:27; 23:10; 23:14; Mic. 1:7).

While the prophetic accusation of "harlotry" had a literal reference to the sacred prostitution of the Baal cult, it extended its meaning by metaphor into the entire theology of worship. It referred to worship that sought fulfillment through self-expression, worship that accepted the needs and desires and passions of the worshiper as its raw material. "Harlotry" is worship which says, "I will give you satisfaction. You want religious feelings? I will give them to you. You want your needs fulfilled? I'll do it in the form most attractive to you."

The divine will which sets itself in opposition to the tastes, preoccupations and perceptions of humanity is incomprehensible in Baalism and so is impatiently discarded. Baalism is worship reduced to the spiritual stature of the worshiper. Its canons are that it should be interesting, relevant, and exciting.

Yahwism established a form of worship which was centered in the proclamation of the word of the covenant God. The appeal was made to the will. Humankind's rational intelligence was roused to attention as it was called upon to respond as a person to the will of God. In Yahwism something was *said*—words which called men and women to serve, love, obey, act responsibly, decide.

In contrast to Baalism, Yahwism exerted continuous pressure to elevate worship into the sphere of conscious intelligence and clearly defined concepts. In Israel, worship was not just the work of the priest by himself; he was joined by the prophet and the prophetic word was incorporated into the temple worship. Israel in its maturity had a worship dominated by the prophetic word of God.

Worship in Israel was no sideline. It sought, and to a great extent succeeded, in achieving authentic expression of a living religion that penetrated the whole of human life. It caught up the personal, the spiritual, and the national life at the same time as it gathered the physical side of life (buildings and bodies) as media for its proclamation of God's word.

God's covenant word initiated and controlled worship, but sensory participation was not excluded. There were bodily actions of kneeling and prostration in prayer. Sacred dances and antiphonal singing expressed community solidarity. The garb of priests and the stylized preparation of sacrifices developed dramatic energies. Solemn silence accompanied the offering of the holy gifts to God and sensitized ears to listen. Clouds of incense billowing up from the altar gave a sensory expression to prayer. Human beings were taken seriously in their totality as psychosomatic beings. The sensory life was given its due in the relationship with God. But as rich and varied as it was, it was a part defined and controlled by the word of God. Nothing was done simply for the sake of the sensory experience involved. There is the "complete penetration and exposition of the cultus by the spoken word, in which is established the supremacy of the individual person's spiritual relation to God over the sacramental experience of God."[29]

The distinction between the worship of Baal and the worship of Yahweh is a distinction between approaching the will of the covenant God which could be understood and known and obeyed, and the blind life-force in nature which could only be felt, absorbed, and imitated. The sexual-orgiastic complex which was bound up with the magic and divinization of nature was always a temptation and frequently a snare, but it was consistently rejected by the community as a whole and by its prophetic leaders.

Pastors are subjected to two recurrent phrases from the people to whom they give spiritual leadership. Both are reminiscent of Baalism, enough so as to earn the label, "Neo-Baalism." The phrases are: "Let's have a worship experience" and "I don't get anything out of it."

The phrase "let's have a worship experience" is Baalism's substitute for "let us worship God." The difference is between cultivating something that makes sense to an individual and acting in response to what makes sense to God. In a "worship experience," a person sees something which excites interest and tries to put religious wrappings around it. A person experiences something in the realm of dependency, anxiety, love, and a connection is made with the ultimate. Worship is a movement from what a person sees, or experiences, or hears, to prayer or celebration or discussion in a religious atmosphere. Subjectivity is encouraged.

But neither Bible nor church uses the word "worship" as a description of experience. Pastors hear this adjectival usage in sentences like, "I can have a worship experience with God on the golf course." That means, "I have religious feelings reminding me of good things, awesome things, beautiful things nearly any place." Which is true enough. The only thing wrong with the statement is its ignorance, thinking that such experiences make up what the church calls "worship." The biblical usage is very different. It talks of worship as a response to God's word in the context of the community of God's people. Worship is neither subjective only nor private only. It is not what I feel when I am by myself; it is how I act toward God in responsible relation with God's people. Worship, in the biblical sources and in liturgical history, is not something a person *experiences,* it is something we *do,* regardless of how we feel about it, or whether we feel anything about it at all. Experience develops out of worship. Isaiah saw, heard, and felt on the day he received his call while at worship in the Temple—but he didn't go there in order to have a "seraphim experience."

The one place where we know that "worship experience" was encouraged was in Baalism. When you were terror-stricken you offered a sacrifice; when you were anxious about the crops you made a visit to the temple prostitute; when you were joyful you ingested the wine god. You did what you felt like doing when you felt like doing it. In between, you got on with your ordinary life. Feelings called the tune, feelings of panic, of terror, of desire, of enthusiasm. Baalism provided a rich array of "worship experiences."

Israel and the Christian church insisted that worship was the proclamation of the will of God and the call for human response to it. The word was authoritative and clear. Nothing was dependent on feelings or weather. All was determined by scripture. No person was left to do what he or she felt like doing. The "shape of the liturgy" gave shape to their lives.[30] God revealed his nature and demanded obedience to it. Worship was the act of attending to that revelation and being obedient to it.

The other phrase of "neo-Baalism" is "I don't get anything out of it." When it refers to participation in the Christian community it is accepted as a serious criticism and a valid excuse from further engagement in something which personal experience testifies is ir-·relevant and uninteresting.

The assumption that supposedly validates the phrase is that worship must be attractive and personally gratifying. But that is simply Baalism *redivivus,* worship trimmed to the emotional and spiritual specifications of the worshiper. The divine will which declares something beyond or other than what is already a part of the emotional-mental construct of the worshiper is spurned. That worship might call for something *beyond* us is shrugged off as obscurantist.

And so the one indispensable presupposition of Christian worship, the God of the covenant who reveals himself in his word, is deleted. A Freudian pleasure principle is substituted and worship is misused to harness God to human requirements. Worship is falsified into being a protective cover for self-seeking. That the self-seeking is in the area of the psychic rather than the sexual does little to improve the results over the old Baalism. We may be entertained, warmed, diverted, or excited in such worship; we will probably not be changed, and we will not be saved. Our feelings may be sensitized and our pleasures expanded. But our morals will be dulled and our God fantasized.

This does not mean that the person who comes to worship must put up with anything, however incompetent and banal, that is offered from chancel and pulpit. Nor does it mean that the person who leads worship does not need to attend to the emotionally felt needs of those who come. The word of God must be "truly preached and the sacraments rightly administered." There must be provision for adequate praise, and for prayers both intimate and intelligent. Pastor and people have complementary responsibilities in both providing for and participating in such acts of worship. When they do, there will be no lack of vital experience, for authentic, biblical worship is endlessly creative. It is difficult to imagine bored psalm-singers straggling up the steps of the Solomonic Temple. It is unlikely that the apostolic preaching put many persons (besides Eutychus!) to sleep.

"The End of the Matter . . . Fear God"

Ecclesiastes is the Old Testament equivalent to the New Testament's empty tomb. The empty tomb, a story that the canonical gospels agree is essential for understanding the resurrection, is the experience of a great no. It represents what humanity does not have to, in fact, cannot, do. I don't have to take care of God; he can take care of himself. I don't have to watch over his body; I don't have to protect him from his enemies; I don't have to manage him, defend him, or tell him what needs to be done next. The tomb is empty—which means that I can go home and go about the work to which I have been called and commanded.

John and Peter ran to the tomb because they supposed that it had been either plundered or desecrated. Mary had reported that the stone had been removed and without bothering to look inside gave her hurried report to the men who assumed the commonplace—graverobbing. Graverobbing was common in that day. Corpses were wrapped in expensive spices (Jesus had been buried by a very rich man, Joseph of Arimethea) and so a corpse was an attractive object for plunder. Or, the body could have been stolen out of malice. The same cruel persons who had managed the crucifixion could have continued their work in desecrating the body. Either or both of these possibilities would have been in the minds of John and Peter as they ran to the tomb. They were in love with Jesus and full of the highest and bravest motives. They ran to interrupt the robbers or to apprehend the desecrators.

When they arrived the grave was empty. Yet, not completely empty: the grave clothes were there with the head napkin folded separately. John observed the evidence, made some rapid deductions (should he not be honored as the patron saint of all detectives?) and came to a conclusion: "he saw and believed." (John 20:8) Believed what? Believed that *God* was at work. He knew that neither

robbers nor desecrators had been at work. Robbers would have left
the grave-wrappings after they ripped them from the body in the
search for valuable spices. There would have been a mess. Desecrators would have left nothing at all, removing the body in its wrappings. But the wrappings were intact and the headcloth neatly
folded. What John had expected to see he did not see—he expected
to see the evidence of humanity's sin; he saw the evidence of God's
power. And what he expected to do he did not do. He expected to
rescue the body, to preserve the dignity of death, to apprehend the
robbers or the desecrators. But God had already taken care of himself.

The persons with whom pastors work (and pastors themselves
are not excepted) carry around a great deal of moral and religious
baggage which is no part of the gospel at all. We work very hard at
our faith; we agonize over it; we struggle with it; we grimly and
determinedly set our jaws to make it through. The empty tomb is
a monument against that. Persons active in religious leadership very
often become patronizing to God, treating him as someone we must
take care of. We think that what we do determines his effectiveness,
and fail to see that that is the position of a pagan towards an idol,
not a creature bowed before the Creator.

Until the crucifixion Jesus, with his authoritative healings and
teachings, had been indisputably in control. But the crucifixion was
so extreme that the disciples felt that they had to take over. Jesus had
got himself into such a fix that those who loved and served him
needed to rescue him through acts of embalming, acts of mourning,
acts of defense. But when they got to the tomb they found that they
were wrong. God had done what needed to be done. Charles Williams exposes the futility of all the people in the history of the church
who have been just a little "too ardent . . . on behalf of the Omnipo-
tence."[31] Qoheleth says "The end of the matter [is this] . . . Fear
God." (12:13)

Some editions of the New Testament have the Psalms included
at the end. It is a most appropriate conclusion. The Psalms integrate
the experience of grace into our lives at every level of praise and
petition, of faith and doubt. They express gratitude and struggle for
honesty in confession. The person who comes of age in Christ finds

many ways in which the Psalms nurture the personal intimacies that keep faith fresh and "new every morning." A pastor is as likely to use a Psalm, for both personal renewal and pastoral work, as any other part of the Bible.

In the same way that the Psalms are an appropriate conclusion to the New Testament, Ecclesiastes is an appropriate introduction.[32] People bring so many mistaken expectations to the gospel, so much silly sentiment, and so many petulant demands, that they hardly hear its real message or confront its actual promise. Qoheleth gets rid of all that. He empties us of the inner noise that we supposed was religion and the cluttered piety we supposed was faith. He throws out the accumulated religious junk and banishes the fraud that has paraded as faith.

Placing Qoheleth's well-orchestrated *hebel* (no!) as a preface to the New Testament provides pastoral direction in clearing the air of the distractions and deceits which distort or drown out the gospel message, freeing persons to simply and directly "fear God." It would not, I think, be mistaken for the message. There is no "message" in Ecclesiastes—"With him there can be no talk of a message which he has to deliver, since all that is left for him to do is to warn against illusions."[33] His work is simply to clear away what is mistaken for religion so that we are free to hear the word of God. Martin Luther's high regard for Ecclesiastes derived from this pastoral function—"this noble little book, which for good reasons it were exceedingly worthwhile that it should be read of all men with great carefulness every day"[34] for Luther, along with his colleagues in reformation, knew how necessary it was to demonstrate the vanity of everything, however fine and respected, which was severed from the God of the gospel so that we may realize the emptiness of all words and forms and become responsive to the living God in resurrection. It is essential, albeit unglamorous, pastoral work, for, as Meister Eckhart put it, "No cask holds two kinds of drink at the same time. If the cask is to hold wine, its water must first be poured out, leaving the cask empty and clean. If you are to have divine joy, all your creatures must first be poured out or thrown out."[35]

The
PASTORAL WORK
of
COMMUNITY-BUILDING:
ESTHER

> True community does not come into being because peo-
> ple have feelings for each other (though that is required,
> too), but rather on two accounts: all of them have to
> stand in a living, reciprocal relationship to a single living
> center, and they have to stand in a living, reciprocal
> relationship to one another. The second event has its
> source in the first but is not immediately given with it. A
> living reciprocal relationship includes feelings but is not
> derived from them. A community is built upon a living,
> reciprocal relationship, but the builder is the living, ac-
> tive center.
>
> —Martin Buber[1]

All pastoral work takes place in the setting of the church, the
community of faith. The pastor is never a private chaplain to individuals; the pastor is never an impersonal speaker to crowds; the pastor
is set in community and given the task of building that community.
Such work is applauded on all sides—until the well-wishers realize
that it is a community of *faith* that is being built, at which point they
begin to offer numerous suggestions for doing something else.

Max Weber, the German sociologist, visited America in 1905
and spoke with admiration of the "voluntary associations" which

proliferated on our landscape. He noted that they bridged the transition between the closed hierarchical society of the Old World which was formed under heavy biblical influence, and the fragmented individualism of the New World in which communities had been eroded by competition. He saw how crucial a social function these groupings perform in American life. A standard cliche about American society is that the Americans are "joiners" and "belongers." The derisive attack by Sinclair Lewis on Babbitt who belonged to the Elks, Boosters, and a network of other service clubs and lodges, became a stereotype of American social criticism. It is true that the associative impulse is strong in American life: no other civilization can show as many secret fraternal orders, businessmen's service clubs, trade and occupational associations, social clubs, garden clubs, women's clubs, church clubs, theater groups, political and reform associations, veterans' groups, ethnic societies, and other clusterings of trivial or substantial importance.

All of which is evidence that persons know that they are no longer sufficient unto themselves. We need community to complete our humanity. And yet these secular attempts at community are notoriously void of meaning. American problems seem to feature loneliness. Karen Horney, coming from Germany to America, was compelled to change her whole theory about the neurotic personality when she found how different were the inner sources of conflict in America from those in Germany, and how much of a role loneliness played in American conflicts.

In a society in which there is very little community and in which the "Babbitt" attempts at community fall so far short of providing it, there is a special urgency in pastoral work to nurture communities in which the gospel is shared. But the cultural context in which this pastoral work is done—i.e. the many secular attempts at community —makes it almost certain that such pastoral work will be identified with one or another of these experiences, and therefore confused and misunderstood. The community of faith in which a pastor works is not insulated from and not uninfluenced by the communities of the world. The people with whom we work maintain multiple memberships—not only do they belong to the church; they also belong to the Lions, the Garden Club, and the Committee on Fair Housing.

Experiences and expectations from these groups are brought over into the community of faith and used for evaluation, planning, and administration, complicating the work enormously, for, as Karl Barth has observed, "the Christian community . . . is an alien colony for the nature and existence of which there are no analogies in the world around, and therefore no categories in which to understand it, and therefore no real use."[2]

So if there is a generalized respect for the pastor in his or her work as a builder of a community of faith, there are also specific distractions from the work and surprisingly insistent pressures to do something quite different. For a community of faith, it turns out, is the least utilitarian grouping of persons on earth, and its essential nature less self-evident than any other category of persons. The church cannot even exhibit what many suppose to be its obvious *raison d'etre,* a clear demonstration of goodness in advance of the cultural religion (or irreligion) of the unchurched populace. For when it comes down to actual cases the level of observable virtue in a church is probably no higher than in an ornithological club, and may be lower.

F. S. C. Northrop (in *The Meeting of East and West*) takes the deepest thing about any civilization to be its metaphysic—its assumptions and beliefs about the constitution of the unseen universe, and he suggests that it was the reception by America of the atomistic metaphysics of Locke and Hume which has influenced the individualism and fragmentation of American life. Pastoral work which has accepted, uncritically, this cultural heritage has found itself with a view of the human being that is individualistic and atomistic. For the American is a person without a community—part of a crowd not of a group. David Reisman explored the American character in terms of its submission to the tyranny of crowds and the failure of the individuals to heal their loneliness in the crowd. Pastoral work is interested in people and their failure to achieve the humanity which is theirs by the will of the God who created them. The pastor who works with such people sees them not as a unicellular organism but as "members of the body."

Even deeper in the American past than its tradition of frontier individualism are old biblical memories embedded in the lives of people. These memories are accessible for identification and are stronger (because truer) than the veneer of Locke and Hume. These memories recall the essential reality of humanity as corporate. In the Genesis story of creation Adam was not complete until there was Eve. The meaning is clear enough: no individual is complete in himself, in herself; humanity is person-in-relationship. Persons are always part of community even when they deny it, even when they don't know it. The congregation *(qahal)* is the basic working unit in God's relations with the Hebrew people. To be cut off from the community was the worst punishment in their legal system. An individual, forced to exist alone in exile, was not a whole person. There are no Robinson Crusoe traditions in the biblical narratives. You could be damned by yourself but you could not be saved by yourself. Ministry that singles persons out from the crowd and addresses them as if they were entities in themselves, treating them as solitary monads in the universe, reduces them to something less than the way they are treated in the Bible. The biblical view of man and woman is person-in-community, a "people of God."

The American tradition of individualism has interposed itself between pastoral work and the biblical heritage. The myth of the self-sufficient individual permeates the American self-consciousness. When these individuals get together in crowds the myth is simply accentuated, for the crowd is not a company but an aggregate, a multiplication of individuals rather than an organic body. Even in the crowd each person is an individual.

In the New Testament the energies of ministry that flow around and across the Mediterranean, that "blue pool in the old garden," bring churches into being, not simply individual Christians. John A. T. Robinson in his classic study of Pauline anthropology, *The Body,* notes,

> The flesh-body was not what partitioned a man off from his neighbour; it was rather what bound him in the bundle of life with all men and nature, so that he could never make his unique answer to God as an isolated individual, apart from his relation to his neighbour.[3]

Instead of a mass of individuals, pebbles in a box, there was a consciousness of being one body, an individual in Christ and members of another. The Christian did not find individuality reduced but personality expanded. Persons who had been turned by Roman census-takers into statistics were initiated into communities of faith in which each person received a new name.

Pastoral work, caught between an American emphasis on the individual and the biblical insistence on community, struggles to find ways to address not single persons but a "people." Men and women must be edged out of their rugged, so-called, individualism in order to experience the wholeness of the gospel which redeems whole persons in community of faith.

The work is difficult and fraught with misunderstandings. The church (in America, at least) is treated with politeness and credited with being an asset to the community as a whole. This general community goodwill is reflected in the legislation that exempts churches from taxation. The clear consensus of the nation is that having churches around is a good thing. The various persons that pastors meet in the course of their work express this generalized but unfocused consensus that the church is good for something: advertisers want to use the church as a market for their products, political organizations want to use the church's concern for justice as a means of support; ecclesiastical bureaucracies want to strengthen the congregation as a foundation under the high-rise structures of institutionalism. Within a brief span of time I made notes on calls from the promoter of a new bowling alley, asking me to organize a team from my congregation ("because I know, Pastor, how interested you are in getting people together in ways that will help them work out their conflicts in healthy ways—and there is no more American way than through sports"); from the chairperson of the local cancer society who wanted me to arrange to call every woman in the parish in regard to a pap test ("because I know of your deep pastoral concern for your parishioners"); from a representative of a church pictorial directory company ("to help your people get to know each other, because that's what it's all about in the church, isn't it?") and from a church leader in my denomination asking me to bring several persons from my congregation to an overnight workshop on developing a budget and raising money ("because we're trying to support you by strengthening your leadership where it counts").

Each of the attempts to use my pastoral leadership in a community of Christians was well-intentioned. The motives of the persons calling were, as far as I know, exemplary and what they were proposing to do was useful. I would unhesitatingly agree that each was doing worthwhile, and, in some cases, admirable work. But I said no to each of them. I was, I hope, courteous in my refusals. In two instances I referred the caller to a person in the congregation to work with, but encountered resistance—it was the high visibility and influence of *my* position that was wanted. So I was misunderstood by all, I did not represent what a church ought to be; I did not comply with the expectations of those who "knew" what the church was there for and were acting on their knowledge.

The plain fact is that the community of faith, the church, is a highly specialized community. It has a unique character. It is not a jack-of-all-trades organization, standing around on elm-shaded street corners with the off-chance of being useful to somebody or other. God's people are a community *sui generis*. There is nothing quite like it. No analogies or parallel experiences are adequate to explain its nature.

It would be unthinkable for me to barge into a physician's office and ask him or her personally to distribute tracts on salvation to patients, or to call an attorney's secretary and ask for the attorney's clients to be assembled for me so that I could address them on the ethics of the Sermon on the Mount, yet I have had equivalent requests put to me by them. The difference is that I know what the proper work of a physician and an attorney is, but they don't know mine. Pastoral work, particularly in matters related to church leadership, does not have a definitive profile in the community, and so persons do not think it presumptuous or out of the way to ask us to do whatever they think will be helpful.

All the expectations are good-natured. Most of the requests are kindly meant. Nevertheless, they are noxious to pastoral ministry. If they are assimilated into pastoral work they will ruin it.

Education is not the answer. It is not feasible to re-educate the community at large on the proper role of the pastor in the work of leading a congregation. Misunderstanding is inevitable and is going to continue for, from the outside, the church *does* look very much like many voluntary service organizations. But it is feasible for pastors to acquire a clear and confident understanding of their own work so that they will be able to tell the difference between what God has set them to do in the church and what others ask them to do, and the presence of mind to say yes to the one and no to the other.

Purim

In the search for biblical orientation in giving leadership to the community of faith, pastoral attention is attracted to the book of Esther because it presents the issue of the nature and function of God's people in stark and simple terms: survival versus annihilation. Is it possible for a community of faith to exist at all in an alternately indifferent and hostile world? Can a community of faith prevail on the simple grounds of being God's people?—without demonstrating usefulness to the society in general, and without access to power in that society?

This basic, either/or question is answered with a resounding affirmative in the Esther story, and then celebrated noisily in the Feast of Purim. The people of God were threatened with destruction. They were not destroyed. The experience was not unlike that undergone by Dostoyevsky when he faced the prospect of execution and was at the last moment reprieved; the presence of death heightened all aspects of life, gave them deeper color, new reality. One becomes conscious of the basic miracle of minimal being in such crisis situations.

And so they celebrate. God acted to preserve the community, his people. The result was a wildly celebrative joy. Purim, an annual feast in the early spring, is characterized by rejoicing and thanksgiving. There are exchanges of gifts between friends and charity to the poor. Life together is celebrated as a joyous gift, snatched unbelievably from the gates of death and hell. A people who had faced the possibility of not being are emphatically alive. Community is not explained in historical terms, it is not analyzed in sociological terms, it is *enjoyed* in the language and rituals and food and laughter of a festival.

Among Jews, still, the family festival meal held on the late afternoon of Purim is second in importance only to that of the Seder service at Passover.[4] The book itself, Esther, is the one "most beloved and well known by the Jews."[5] Maimonides, the medieval Jewish theologian, put the book of Esther at the very top of the sacred writings and taught that when all else passed away, the Law and Esther would remain. The reason for this high regard is that Esther celebrates the eternal miracle of the survival of God's people.

Purim continues to be the gayest of all the Jewish holidays. There is merrymaking, feasting, and drinking. The rabbis had a saying that although moderation is required throughout the year, on Purim it was permitted to drink wine "until you didn't know the difference between blessed be Mordecai and cursed be Haman." In modern Israel Purim is now called, after this rabbinic saying, *Ad lo yadat,* "until you can't tell the difference. . . ." It is a kind of Mardi-gras, with parades, dancing, partying, and feasting. It is a yearly rebuke to the dour institutionalism caricatured in Ellen Glasgow's *The Sheltered Life:* ". . . Old Mortality, a green bullfrog with a Presbyterian face, sat on a moss-grown log in the midst of a few faded lily-pads and croaked prophetically, at twilight, of the evil to come."[6]

By telling the story of the survival of the faith-community and commanding its yearly celebration in the feast of Purim, Esther continues to be an important document for pastoral work, defining the setting in which community is shaped, ruled, and preserved by God in the context of praise.

Joy is not an individual stroke of good luck. It is a community participation in God's redemption:

> . . . the city of Susa shouted and rejoiced. The Jews had light and gladness and joy and honor. And in every province and in every city, wherever the king's command and his edict came, there was gladness and joy among the Jews, a feast and a holiday. (8:15–16).

If we are found beautiful, if we are permitted to live for another day, if we escape hate and rejection, it is because of the mercy and providence of God.

Salvation is not only individual; it is corporate. In the corporateness, and because of it, there is joy. Joy is not a private emotion, it requires community for both its development and expression. And since the community is provided and preserved by God, the response is joy in God.

> Singers and dancers alike say,
> "All my springs are in you!" (Ps. 87:7)

Pastoral concern in this area has to do with the ease with which the experience of joy is separated from the God who wills that " 'my joy may be in you, and that your joy may be full.' " (John 15:11) Joy, separated from its roots in God and pursued apart from the community of faith, becomes mere sensation. It is as easy to separate experiences of joy from God as it is to separate experiences of suffering from God. If the result of the latter is bitterness, the result of the former is boredom—ennui. Our culture has appointed the entertainment and leisure industries as guides to the experience of joy. But they are blind guides. The pastor works among persons who define joy as a way of buying something they want or trying out a new sensation. Even events that carry natural and spontaneous joys with them—the birth of a child, witnessing a marriage, moving into a new home, getting a new job, graduating from a school—are commercialized and banalized. People hear the message that God gives joy, and they know that joy is possible, but they lack skills for enjoyment. Hearing the message of joy they run out to buy a toy instead of joining the party that God is giving. The culture preaches and promises joy ("pursuit of happiness" is doctrinal orthodoxy in the American way of life), but it sets it in a context which is private and secular, something I get for myself at the expense of others, and something I get apart from my relation with God. "Our culture," writes Henri Nouwen, "is a working, hurrying, and worrying culture with many opportunities except the opportunity to celebrate life."[7]

The two themes, the indisputable *fact* of the community and the irrepressible *feast* of the community, are interwoven in the story and the festival. The story of the survival of the community is told; the joyous festival is celebrated. Esther and Purim, the story and the feast, are two parts of the same thing, namely, the community of faith. They must not be separated. If the festival is isolated from the story, that is, if the attempt to celebrate is separated from the reason for celebration, the party quickly degenerates into a celebration of life as a thing in itself, an adoration of the life-force. It then becomes either a jingoistic parade of racism or nationalism (community hardened into institutionalism), or a carnival indulgence of sensuality (community disintegrated into an orgy). D. H. Lawrence, who tried the alternatives, wrote that "Men are free when they belong to a living, organic, *believing* community, active in fulfilling some unfulfilled, perhaps unrealized purpose. Not when they are escaping to some wild west."[8] By rooting its understanding and expression of community in the book of Esther, pastoral work avoids the rigidities of imposed totalitarianism on the one hand, and the formlessness of a free-for-all anarchism on the other. Esther and Purim provide a model for exhibiting the celebrative existence of a people who freely share and exchange God's gifts of created and redeemed life together. It is the story and feast of what is discussed in theological terms under the heading *communio sanctorum,* the communion of the saints.

Susa

The story of Esther is set in the Persian city of Susa in the fifth century B.C., which puts it at the far edge, both geographically and chronologically, of Old Testament biblical history. One hundred and fifty miles southwest of Susa and fourteen hundred years earlier, Abraham had set out from Ur and traveled westwards, following the arc of the fertile crescent, all the way to Egypt. He personally paced off nearly the whole of the territory on which the biblical story would be lived out over the next two thousand years. God's call to Abraham began with a promise that he would be the founder of a great community of faith:

> Now the LORD said to Abram, "Go from your country and your kindred and your father's house to the land that I will show you. And I will make . . . your name great, so that you will be a blessing. I will bless those who bless you, and him who curses you I will curse; and by you all the families of the earth will bless themselves." (Gen. 12:1–3)

After several generations of nomadic, tribal existence, mostly in Palestine in the person of Abraham and his descendants, the Hebrew people came into being in Egypt in such a way as to be recognizable as a *nation*. The familiar story of their slavery under the pharaohs, their deliverance under Moses, the shaping of a spiritual and social identity at Sinai, and the formation of a common life of faith in the years of wilderness wandering is definitive in understanding a community of faith. The seven centuries that followed under the rule of judges and kings continue the story, filling in details and elaborating earlier themes, furnishing the mind with the historical stuff of the actual experience of being God's people. These narrations only indirectly provide a history of ancient Hebrew tribes who became the "children of Israel," and only tangentially provide evidence for Bronze and Iron Age civilizations. The documents are not naive primitive traditions waiting to be probed for significance by recently acquired insights into the structure of folk myths. Nor are they skeleton outlines waiting to be rearranged into a respectable history by utilizing the wealth of material provided by recent archaeological discoveries. They are, as is, complete in themselves, a comprehensive presentation of a *community* of faith, a *people* of God.

Across the span of those centuries, rubbing shoulders with four or five different cultures, these people learned to understand themselves as a people created, provided for, ruled, and redeemed by God. They told stories, worshiped, praised, sacrificed, sang, preached, and prayed. There were massive acts of disobedience and rebellion; there were marvelous returns in repentance and renewal. But through it all there is a continuous awareness that they were a spiritually unique, corporate reality (not a race, not a government, not a culture) shaped by God's call and rule.

The forms of their corporate life changed: they were slaves in Egypt, refugees in Sinai, loosely knit tribes in Canaan, a splendid and energetic monarchy, survivors of a civil war. Always, though, they were God's people, descendants of Abraham's seed and somehow, even though darkly, an instance of God's blessing and the means by which the nations of the earth "will bless themselves."

Then, quite suddenly, they were a captive people again, conquered by the Babylonians who were soon succeeded by the Persians. They spent the next several centuries uprooted from the land they had come to identify as their own, separated from the worship in Jerusalem that had centered their common life for nearly half a millennium, and dispersed across the fertile crescent to all points of the compass. Two Jewish communities, one at Elephantine in southern Egypt, the other at Susa in Persia, span geographically the vast area in which the Jews experienced life together throughout this time of dispersion.[9] Not much is known of either outpost colony. The Elephantine Jews are not mentioned in the Bible, their existence only coming to light through the discovery of some Aramaic papyri in 1911.[10] The Susa Jews, unmentioned in any historical sources, are known only from the biblical story of Esther. The period itself, the fifth century B.C. is, strangely, more obscure than any other in biblical history, with very little in the way of archaeological, linguistic, or documentary material to use in reconstructing the history of the times.[11] But the very paucity of the evidence, on the one hand meager and on the other uninspired, invites reflection: the elimination of detail and background leaves a kind of stark black-and-white picture of what is basic: a surviving community of faith.

These glimpses of the Old Testament community of faith coming towards the end of the biblical period in many ways parallel those which came at the beginning. The Hebrews began as wanderers and captives. They end similarly. In Esther, the people who in the early pages of the Hebrew Bible are shown to be formed in an environment of Egyptian hostility, are shown surviving the machinations of a Persian pogrom in the last pages. Gillis Gerleman has pointed out many similarities between the Exodus and Esther narratives. These involve matters of style, the way in which various characters are depicted, as well as the handling of various details in the narratives. It seems clear that the Jews in Susa took the Israelites in Egypt as their model. They are a community of faith because, and only because, of God's saving act.[12]

From the Elephantine papyri we can construct a fairly detailed picture of a Jewish community flourishing far from its origins in Jerusalem, surviving the pressures of erosion and assimilation in a strange culture, and emerging intact from at least one episode of active persecution. But one of the things that is clear from the papyri is that this Jewish colony practiced a religion that was highly syncretistic: in addition to worshiping Yahweh they included the deities

Eshem-bethel, Herem-bethel, and 'Anath-bethel. Even if these were intended as designations for qualities of Yahweh, as some scholars think, still the practice is heterodox. Also, quite contrary to Deuteronomic law, they had a temple to Yahweh with an altar on which burnt offerings and sacrifices were offered.

> It appears from this that the Jews of Elephantine, although not overt polytheists, had combined a highly unorthodox Yahwism with features drawn from syncretistic cults of Aramean origin. Though calling themselves Jews and feeling kinship . . . with their brethren in Palestine, they by no means stood in the main stream of Israel's history and faith.[13]

But even though they had developed "a somewhat questionable type of Jewish faith under pagan influence,"[14] they were in apparently good standing with the restoration Jews in Palestine, getting funds and instructions from them for rebuilding their destroyed temple.

The Susa and Elephantine instances of faith communities are important for pastoral work inasmuch as neither demonstrates a community at its best. Neither is a "model" congregation. These are not flourishing instances of what it means to be God's people. They are far removed from the Davidic golden age. They are scarce in both holiness and piety. The colony at Elephantine had mixed pagan forms of worship into its heritage, and practiced a flawed and compromised kind of community. There is no record of the Jewish community in Susa even mentioning the name of God during its time of greatest stress. Neither community is admirable—but both are *facts*. They are evidence of the survival of a faith community, despite themselves, against all odds. The community is reduced to a bare existence, yet *existing*. The community survives not because of its theological purity (for Elephantine was far from pure) nor for its moral piety (of which there is very little in Esther), but because of God's grace.

The faith community is everywhere and always a creation of God the Spirit. There is no evidence that this or that form of government provides better or worse conditions for living together as a community of faith. Outwardly difficult times may, in fact, be propitious. There was a tradition in Israel that remembered the time of the wilderness as the honeymoon period of their corporate life. In the eighth century, a time of economic prosperity but spiritual decadence, Hosea remembered when things were different—when bare economic survival was accompanied by spiritual wealth. He represented God as saying:

> ". . . I will allure her,
>   and bring her [back] into the wilderness,
>   and speak tenderly to her.
> And there I will give her her vineyards,
>   and make the Valley of Achor a door of hope.
> And there she shall answer as in the days of her youth,
>   as at the time when she came out of the land of Egypt.
> "And in that day, says the LORD, you will call me, 'My
>   Ba'al.' " (Hos. 2:14–16)

In other words, "I will take you back to the place where you first discovered what it meant to live in a covenant of love with God, back into those wilderness years. There, stripped down to the essentials, we will find out what it means to be saved and loved. Undistracted by the trappings of ease, luxury, we will have time simply to pay attention to each other." Return to the wilderness became synonomous with getting back to the basics. In the light of that tradition it is possible to see the Persian diaspora as a kind of wilderness experience.

The pastoral imagination that is oriented in this history will be quick to spot essentials and sense what is foundational. It will develop a *theological* understanding of the community of faith as opposed to a sociological, or even historical understanding. It will understand the people of God as a grouping of persons whom God has called together, whom God will keep together, who will survive by God's grace. It will not understand them as a group of people who attempt to be religious together.

Every so often a magazine article appears reporting the results of a survey taken among persons who go to church. The pollster asks, "Why do you go to this church?" and gets a variety of trivial answers: "I want my children to learn Bible stories"; "I like the preacher—he preaches love and not hellfire and brimstone"; "There is an early service and so we can still have most of the day to go sailing." "It is the closest church," etc. Rarely, if ever, does anyone respond, "Because God called me," and yet that is the real reason. Every gathering of the people begins with a call to worship. People assemble for worship because God called them together whether they know it or not.

The pastoral understanding of community that is thoroughly immersed in this long, biblical tradition and comprehends the biblical dynamics of grace, will not be quickly impressed with comparative statistics which judge the church by its visibility in the world or its impact on the census tables, and then be distracted into ventures of titanism and multitudinism. From a biblical point of view it is hard to conceive of a method for describing or understanding or evaluating the church which is less likely to get even a glimpse of its reality than those devised by statisticians or sociologists. Yet these persons provide the bulk of the material that is used to exhort the pastor in his or her work as a leader in the community of faith.

There is, of course, nothing wrong with a large-membership congregation. But neither is there anything right about it. Size is not a moral quality. It is a given. It is what is there—part of the environment in which the pastor works. "It is not the pastor's fault if he is born in times of barrenness, when it is difficult to do good."[15] Size is mostly the result of cultural conditions. Congregations are large when there is social approval to be part of a religious establishment, small when there isn't. The pastor cannot choose his or her culture. The size of the congregations we serve is contingent on what decade we happen to be living in and what qualities of leadership happen to be in vogue at the time. While pious ways in the pastor will attract churchgoers in one place, worldly sophistication will attract them in another place. Angry preaching will be rewarded at one time, kindly preaching at another, quite apart from whether either the anger or the kindness communicates the gospel of Jesus Christ. Because these variables are notoriously inconstant, spiritual and biblical integrity is far more important than the skillful use of propaganda in doing pastoral work, the doctrine of providence of more significance than any image-making publicity.

The pastor has no responsibility for the time in history in which he or she does his or her work in the faith community, or, for the most part the particular geographical setting of the work. Pastoral work (or its Israelite equivalent) was conducted in Egyptian Memphis when Ramses II was Pharaoh, in Palestinian Shiloh in the time of the Judges, in Jerusalem when Hezekiah was king, and along the river Chebar in sixth-century Babylonia. Political, economic, social, and cultural conditions were extremely varied in those settings. But to certain persons in each of those times and places was given the task of providing leadership to the community of God's people. The different conditions required differing skills and emphases, but at no time did the leader create the community—it was given to him or her. The leader was a steward in an environment of grace where God's acts were remembered and celebrated, where God's commandments were learned and obeyed, where God's praises were sung and enjoyed. No leader—not Moses, not Samuel, not Isaiah, not Ezekiel—was ever responsible for either the formation or the survival of the community of faith. *That* took place in the counsels of God and by the mercy of God.

Because they understood that, the biblical leaders in the community seemed to be free of the anxiety that is an epidemic among today's pastors: anxiety over survival, worry over size, an obsession with arithmetic. There was no time when things were more desperate than when the Persian pogram, narrated in Esther, was about to be launched. But there was not a trace of panic in Mordecai. He knew what, centuries later, Samuel Rutherford knew, that "It is our Lord's wisdom, that His Kirk should ever hang by a thread; and yet the thread breaketh not, being hanged upon Him who is the sure Nail in David's house, (Isa. xxii.23)."[16] Even though he saw in Esther the only chance of reprieve, his world was not reduced to trusting in her or depending upon her. He is relentless in facing her with her responsibilities but relaxed in contemplating her possible failure of nerve: " 'For if you keep silence at such a time as this, relief and deliverance will rise for the Jews from another quarter, but you and your father's house will perish. And who knows whether you have not come to the kingdom for such a time as this?' " (Esther 4:14) Mordecai faces her with her task; but he also tells her that if she does not choose to accept it, God will find another way. He confronts but he does not bully. He directs but does not devise contingency plans behind the scenes.

Nothing in pastoral work is more liable to Pelagian tendencies than the work of giving leadership to the community of faith. Salvation *sola fide* may be preached faithfully from the pulpit, but during the week a hustling, anxious, frenetic spirit insinuates itself into the routines and vitiates the message. The evil spirit is sloganized into cliches from once grand words like "stewardship," "evangelism," "mission," and then used to legitimize the crassest kind of bitch-goddess nonsense. British pastor Erik Routley, after spending a few months in the United States, wrote of "the staggering and indeed terrifying success mystique of American Protestant churchmanship."[17] A mind steeped in the stories of Abraham and Elephantine, of Exodus and Esther, will be coolly dismissive of the bulk-mail exhortations that flow like a rolling stream across the pastor's desk with breathless suggestions of success in developing a growing church (which always seems to mean a lot more people crowded together under one roof). Cut off from the biblical stories, separated from these traditions and truths, we are alternately set aquiver by every public relations pitch and cast down by the latest sociological analysis. The plain biblical fact is that it makes no difference whether a community of faith numbers thirty-seven persons or thirty-seven hundred. Each soul is of eternal value, and needs to live with a few other souls in order to grow in grace and charity. The pastors' task is to guide the growth of the thirty-seven (if that is where they find themselves) or the thirty-seven hundred (if that be the place) by leading in prayers, preaching God's word, and administering abilities and aptitudes of the Spirit so that ministry takes place. The plain biblical fact is that it makes no difference if there are ten persons in a cavernous gothic city church or five hundred persons crowded into a suburban barn. It is the kind of difference between tenth-century Jerusalem and seventh-century Samaria—the communities contrast in size and condition but are constituted by the same means (the Holy Spirit) and require the same ministries (worship, prayer, teaching, preaching). Advertising techniques, promotional budgets, and organizational charts are bagatelles in such work. They are, it is argued, useful tools to assist the pastoral work. In fact they are enormous distractions. They absorb, like giant sponges, the energies which ought to go into prayer; they dilute concentration in worship; they clutter preaching. The results are often financially pleasing and organizationally satisfying, but the consequences for the faith community are sad, for the essential work of community-building has been abandoned. Ezekiel's lament headlines the disaster: " 'My sheep were scattered over all the face of the earth, with none to search or seek for them.' " (Ezek. 34:6)

Knowledge of and appreciation for the minimum communities of faith at Susa and Elephantine prevent us from idealizing the church. For it is always a mistake to think of the church as a subspecies of utopia. (Martin Thornton thinks that our average congregation is "somewhere near the middle of the book of Judges.")[18] If the congregation is conceptualized in ideal terms, the imperfect reality that we in fact live with must always be addressed in the tiresome, pummeling language of urgent exhortation ("we *must* become what we are called to be!"). The fact is that the community already is what God has brought into being. The Bible, Hans Küng writes, does not begin by " 'laying down a doctrine of the Church which has to be worked out in practice; it starts with the Church as reality, and reflection upon it comes later. The real Church is first and foremost . . . an historical event.' "[19] Then and now. It follows that the ordinary pastoral language used in addressing what is there, already, by God's act, will be in the indicative not the subjunctive—dealing with what God has created by grace not what we must become by sweaty, moralistic exertion.

"In one of George MacDonald's books, there is a woman who has met a sudden sorrow. 'I wish I'd never been made!' she exclaims petulantly and bitterly: to which her friend quietly replies, 'My dear, you're not made yet. You're only being made—and this is the Maker's process.' "[20]

In the fifth century B.C. the Persian empire was a vast sea, including all of what is now Iran, Iraq, Syria, Lebanon, Israel, the Kingdom of Jordan, Egypt, Turkey, as well as parts of Greece and the Balkans, Soviet Russia, Afghanistan, and Pakistan.[21] Scattered throughout that immensity there were numerous, tiny, powerless, apparently insignificant faith communities like Susa and Elephantine. Some no doubt complained that what was on display was unsatisfactory, unworthy instances of the kingdom of God. The answer to the complaint can only be that they were not, and are not, yet made—only *being* made. The fact is that decimated and dispersed as they were, they were *not* swallowed up in the ocean of pagan power and culture and religion. They survived. By grace. The empire did not.

Every church community, no matter how small, how deficient in piety, how lacking in works—think of those seven congregations of the Apocalypse!—is a miraculous and precious gift, an instance, no matter how obscure or flawed, of the kingdom of God, and must, for that reason, be lifted up in thanks. Part of the pastor's work is to lead people in such expressions of gratitude.

With that as a background, no pastor can permit him or herself to be stampeded into leaving the post of prayer and preaching, giving private spiritual direction and leading in public worship, in order to rescue the church from the Philistines, or the Persians, or the Pharisees—or the liberals or fundamentalists or communists. "The lambs of the Good Shepherd were not entrusted to St Peter to be taught, regimented, forced, or neglected, but to be fed."[29]

Haman

At no time in its history did the biblical community of faith exist under more optimum external conditions than during the years of the Persian Empire. Persia was liberal, tolerant, and relaxed with its subject peoples. The official policy was to encourage and strengthen the indigenous cultures and religions in the empire—let them develop in their own ways under their own leadership.[23]

The evidence for this is extensive. For instance, the Passover ordinance of Darius II of the year 419 B.C., found among the papyri of Elephantine, orders that the feast of the Passover and unleavened bread shall be celebrated by the Jewish colony on the island of Elephantine in exact conformity with current regulations. The "important and momentous decree of Cyrus"[24] concerning the rebuilding of the temple also arose in this wide context. The official Aramaic text of the decree is preserved in Ezra 4:3-5, documenting Persia's policy in these matters.

So it is clear that Jews who wished could return to Palestine and Jerusalem—the Persian government would provide resources for rebuilding the Temple and establishing self-rule. Or, if they wished to stay where they were in one of the diaspora exile communities, they were welcome to do that. Many stayed, electing not to return. Excavations at Nippur, southeast of Babylon, and not far from the setting for Esther, have uncovered over seven hundred tablets dating from the fifth century B.C. that are archives from the firm of Murashu Sons, a great Babylonian firm of bankers and brokers. Among other things, Murashu and Sons had a contract to collect taxes for the Persian government in that area. The personal names that appear in the tablets include a large number of Hebrew names, evidence that exiles from Judah had settled in this area. Thus we know that some, after the change of government from Babylonia to Persia, returned to help rebuild Jerusalem while others stayed and entered the social and political and economic life where they were —and prospered. They had prophetic sanction from Jeremiah to follow this plan of action. He had counseled some "to seek the welfare of the city where they were sent, to pray for it and to settle quietly there for a long stay (Jer. 29:1–14)."[25]

These background conditions hold special interest for American pastoral leadership (and, with a few exceptions, for pastors in most of the Western world), for the American tolerance of freedom of religion, including government aid in the development of religious communities (in the form of tax exemptions) is a "right" for which gratitude is often expressed. Cultural congeniality is interpreted as spiritual alliance. But social friendliness is not spiritual consent. The mind that "is enmity against God" (Rom. 8:7, AV) is quite as much a factor under conditions of political and economic freedom as otherwise. The sharp difference between Reinhold Niebuhr and Karl Barth over this issue in 1957 was, perhaps, inconclusive.[26] Niebuhr complained at Barth's failure to speak out against the repressive communist regime in Hungary, implying that the intervention of the Western powers was necessary to free them to serve God better. Barth maintained his silence; his position, spoken quietly to friends and students, was that we Americans had better look to ourselves— that we were in just as much spiritual and moral danger from our affluence as any Eastern European Christian was from persecution. It can, I think, be argued that both Niebuhr's aggression and Barth's restraint can be credited with sharpening our perception of the respective dangers which persecution and tolerance hold for those who do pastoral work.

For it is a fact that it was in the liberal, open, generous Persian environment that the biblical people came to the very edge of extinction. Haman, the Hitler-like villain in the story of Esther, planned the genocide and very nearly succeeded in accomplishing it. He is described as an Agagite (3:1) in contrast to Mordecai, the hero of the Esther story, who is described as a descendant of King Saul (2:5). These designations are a flashback to 1 Samuel 15 and provide the background illumination for understanding the ominous significance of Haman in all matters that concern the survival and development of a biblical community.

Haman was from the tribe of Amalek, a bedouin tribe from the steppes of the deep South. The Amalekites had been Israel's chief enemy during the wilderness wanderings under Moses, when the people of God were in process of formation. It was decreed then that " 'The LORD will have war with Amalek from generation to generation.' " (Exod. 17:16) They were the enemy who first and most obviously sought to deny Israel entry into the promised land. In Deuteronomy they were denounced for having picked off the stragglers from the Israelite column of march. They had come to be regarded as *the* opponents of God's guidance and and providence. So they were far more than one among many military enemies—they were the opponents of *God's* ways. This accounts for the command for their total destruction when King Saul was ordered to " 'smite Amalek, and utterly destroy all that they have; do not spare them, but kill both man and woman, infant and suckling, ox and sheep, camel and ass.' " (1 Sam. 15:3) It is not a people but a way of life that was to be destroyed—a way of life that constituted a powerful and relentless threat to God's rule.

The insight that there is, in fact, an enemy is an important biblical insight for pastoral leadership. This insight is not the same as the sectarian paranoia that sees demons in disease, communists in government, and unbelievers in pulpits. But because some are paranoid does not mean that the demonic is benign, that communists are friends, and that unbelief is harmless. There is danger, and there is threat: there is an enemy. Pastoral work takes place in an environment of hostility. There are times in history when it is overt; other times when it is covert; always it is intense. The pastor who does not know that is unfit to be a guide in the life of the Spirit.

The frequent references in scripture to enemy develop a sensitivity to the fact of opposition and an understanding of its nature. Naivete in regard to evil, especially among those who are called to leadership ministries, is dangerous and provokes the dominical rebuke, "thou mindest not the things of God." (Matt. 16:23, AV) Ringgren in his word-study of the Hebrew noun *'oyebh* (enemy) concludes that the basic biblical use of the word does not refer to the political assailants against Israel, nor to personal difficulties which bring physical suffering and/or spiritual tribulation, but to what is "contrary to God and chaotic."[27] It is, in other words, a theological term, used by a theological community. Foerster in his analysis of the Greek equivalent, *echthros,* comes to a similar conclusion: *"echthros* is particularly used, . . . for what is hostile to God and His Christ."[28]

Wherever there is a people of God there are enemies of God. Pastoral work which seeks to build up the community of faith cannot afford to be innocent about Haman. Only by ignoring the reality and malice of Haman can we suppose that building the community of faith can be accomplished by budgeting for more advertising, by developing better communications, or by training in more sophisticated organizational management. That is like thinking that we can defeat an enemy by infiltrating the front lines under cover of darkness and putting "make love not war" bumper stickers on its tanks, or by using powerful loudspeakers to denounce to them the evil of their ways and proclaim the righteousness of our cause. A *battle* is in progress: that is a biblical fact from Genesis (" 'I will put enmity between . . . your seed and her seed; he shall bruise your head, and you shall bruise his heel' " 3:15), to John (" 'Away with him, away with him, crucify him!' " 19:15), to Revelation ("Now war arose in heaven, Michael and his angels fighting against the dragon" 12:7). There is a battle in which "we are not contending against flesh and blood, but against the principalities, against the powers, against the world rulers of this present darkness, against the spiritual hosts of wickedness in the heavenly places." (Eph. 6:12)

The pastoral responsibilities for building up a community of faith under such conditions are grave and must not be trivialized or secularized: scripture must be taught and preached, prayers must be offered, visitation must be conducted, sacraments must be administered, counsel must be given, worship must be led. There are other ministries to be conducted in both church and world—other weapons to use, other methods of attack—but there are also other persons who are set apart for them. The pastor must do the work *he* or *she* is given to do. The pastor is not the only person involved in ministries that build up the community of faith, but the only one who has *pastoral* work to do. That pastoral work ought to be defined as narrowly as possible to guarantee that it be accomplished expertly and thoroughly.

A realization that there is, in fact, an *enemy* forces a reassessment of priorities. The function of Haman (of Agag, of Satan, of the Beast, et al.) is to force a decision on the "one thing needful." The moment Haman surfaced, Esther began to move from being a beauty queen to becoming a Jewish saint, from being an empty-headed sex symbol to being a passionate intercessor, from the busy-indolent life in the harem to the high-risk venture of speaking for and identifying with God's people.

Pastors who take upon themselves everything that appears worthy of ministry are either unsufferably arrogant, thinking they are the only ones in church capable of hearing commands and of obeying in faith, or else extraordinarily faithless *(oligopistoi!)*[24] who do not give the Holy Spirit credit for being able to lead or direct anyone else. What is required is modesty, the willingness to work within the terms of *pastoral* call, and faith that trusts the Lord of the battle to deploy his servants where and when he wills. If pastors cannot learn such truth from scripture they ought at least to be able to learn it from the mock battle so many of them watch with ritual attention each Sunday afternoon. Any quarterback who became impatient with his blockers and took on those job assignments himself, or who omitted to take the ball from the center and ran out into the secondary as a pass receiver, confident that no one could run pass patterns more expertly than he, would very soon find himself out of a job.

Pastors who do similar things each week keep their jobs only because congregations are more gracious and longsuffering than football fans.

Since Samuel's command to Saul, "utterly destroy," (1 Sam. 15:3) was only partially carried out, it was not carried out at all. By excluding King Agag and the best livestock from destruction, the clear intent of the holy war *(herem)* was violated.[30] God's plans were amended to leave room for just the least bit of royal vanity. The war was commanded by God to remove the threat of a godless and hostile way of life but it was conducted by Saul in terms designed to increase the kingly (read *pastoral*) prestige, showing off Agag as a war prize and dividing the spoils of the plundered livestock among the people. It was Samuel's task to confront Saul, the man whose head he had anointed in affectionate grace (1 Sam. 15:10–16) with God's severe judgment. Samuel's emotions were made up of equal parts of anger and grief. His own counsel had been rejected and his trust violated—and so he was angry. But worse, God's ways had been repudiated and the fate of the people jeopordized—and so he was overwhelmed with grief. In an all-night vigil before the Lord, Samuel pleaded for the sinner as did Abraham for Sodom. All leaders of faith-communities—ancient kings and contemporary pastors—are, directly or indirectly, faced with a similar "severe mercy."[31]

The conversational exchange between Samuel and Saul reads like the verbatim from a confessional: King Saul greets prophet Samuel with hearty and robust cheer, claiming to have acted according to instructions. Samuel confronts him with the evidence of the noisy animals, exposing the falsity of his boast. Saul blames it on the people (" 'they have brought them . . .' " 1 Sam. 15:15) but, at the same time excuses them, since they only did it because they wanted to have animals for offering sacrifices to the Lord. That old sin has had a long life. It is a favorite ploy of pastors still to blame/excuse their congregations. The plain fact was that Saul had consciously misconstrued the nature of his ministry and deliberately rejected God's command. No amount of blaming and excusing could cover that up. Samuel is impatient with his extended and hypocritical rationalization: " 'Stop!' " (1 Sam. 15:16) The issue is completely clear: Saul had assumed control of the kingdom and felt free to give whatever orders he wished. God was now only background: in the day-to-day conduct of affairs Saul took things into his own hands and led the community in whatever way best fed his pride and pleased the people. The will of God was no longer the maker and shaper of the community. The word of God was no longer the center. Saul had taken charge. It was "Saul's church." But he took charge without any sense of the spiritual realities at stake. Under the intoxicating influence of leadership and success he lost sensitivity to both God and the enemy.

> What was required was clear, active obedience, not a hidden non-cooperation. The instrument which the Lord uses must be completely adapted to his hand, and quite dependable. This is the basis for the theological, in other words, the proper and authoritative criticism of King Saul. For this reason, we find here in solemn form the rejection of the man who has rejected the word of God.[32]

When Samuel reviewed the command of God (1 Sam. 15:17–19) all Saul could do was repeat his earlier rationalization (1 Sam. 15:20–21). Harry Stack Sullivan once defined a rationalization as "an exceedingly plausible but highly irrelevant" reason for one's actions. The reasons put forward to explain and justify much pastoral work, especially in areas which have to do with leading congregational growth and development, have a similar ring.

Samuel's indicting words are, in this regard, revealing: " 'Though you are little in your own eyes, are you not the head of the tribes of Israel? The LORD anointed you king over Israel. And the LORD sent you on a mission. . . .' " (1 Sam. 15:17–18) The speech indicates that the root reason for Saul's disobedience was not that he thought too much of himself (that is, that he acted out of arrogance) but that he thought too little of himself (that is, that he was unaware of the importance of all with which God had entrusted him). Pastors are apt to sin out of fear as much as out of pride, out of feelings of inadequacy as much as out of illusions of superiority —not believing the terms of their ordination. An eagerness to display evidence of accomplishment (King Agag, the plundered animals) is symptomatic of a failure to trust God; a timidity in obedience is compensated for by the bold exhibition of trophies.

Pastors who use leadership positions in the community to shore up the ruins of their own ego betray their trust and make work doubly, trebly, difficult for their colleagues and successors. (If Saul had done his job, Mordecai wouldn't have had Haman to deal with.) Statistical applause has nothing to do with faithfulness. A glowing public image has nothing to do with obedience. The prophetic oracle " 'to obey is better than sacrifice' " (1 Sam. 15:22) is a magnificent, clear proclamation of the theme which is later picked up and preached so well by Isaiah (1:11–15), Amos (5:21–27), and Hosea (6:6). It continues to divide those who manipulate the community of faith to serve themselves from those who serve the Lord of the church. The completion by Samuel of the unfinished orders (15: 32–35) re-establishes the rule of God. Saul's leadership is repudiated and he ends an ignoble suicide. In Esther, Haman is hung on his own gallows.

Mordecai

In the Esther story the figure of Haman develops in continuity with the old Amalekite anti-Semite Agag. Mordecai, the descendant of King Saul, is a study in contrast to his ancestor. Saul misjudged his spiritual enemy as a mere foil to his own ambition. He did not recognize the reality of evil and attempted to use the Amalekite in a competitive way to advance himself. He refused to take seriously what God took seriously, taking only himself seriously. He died a crazed suicide. Mordecai, in contrast, was deeply and continuously aware of the spiritual issues at stake, and took a modest and humble role in the affairs with which he had to do. He served anonymously and counseled quietly. The outcome was exaltation. The concluding line in the story is, "For Mordecai the Jew was next in rank to King Ahasuerus, and he was great among the Jews and popular with the multitude of his brethren, for he sought the welfare of his people and spoke peace to all his people." (10:3)

The importance of Mordecai for the pastor derives from his style of leadership, a style that exemplifies the way of the servant. The name Esther gives title to the story but Mordecai is the most important person and carries the leadership role. The very fact that Mordecai's name does not appear in the title is an instance of his servant style. He reared Esther to adulthood; he alertly discovered the assasination plot that saved the king's life; he quietly advised Queen Esther through the Haman crisis. These were acts that took courage, wisdom, skill, and perseverance. He did them all behind the scenes in near anonymity. He betrays no hint of ambition, no *hubris.*

Mordecai is significantly described as "the Jew." Eight times he is thus designated.[33] He was a man of tradition who knew where he had come from and therefore where he was going—"that rooted man."[34] He was singled out for attention when he refused to bow down before Haman's pretentious struts through the city square. That refusal was a quiet consequence of his obedience to the First Commandment. Mordecai was a man of God, in touch with the commandments, whose identity as one of God's people made all other roles secondary. And therefore he was a leader. "When we do not protect with great care our own inner mystery, we will never be able to form community."[35]

His leadership was an outgrowth of what he was: he did not set himself up to lead; he did not aspire to leadership; he was, simply, "a Jew." By living consistently within that identity and doing the duties that went with it he fulfilled the functions of leadership: raising his uncle's daughter, keeping the First Commandment, interceding for his people, trusting in God. Leadership, for Mordecai, was not self-assertion, not ego-fulfillment, but being a man of God and doing whatever flowed naturally from that traditional identity. Daniel Berrigan, who has provided twentieth-century pastoral leadership to a fugitive and underground part of the church, and is often associated with avant-garde ways, says that he sees his task primarily in terms of the difficulty yet necessity of being "a man of tradition."[36]

It is noteworthy that in the one story in the Bible that is given over to narrating the survival of God's people, that the leader most responsible for the survival is a behind-the-scenes-figure known only as "the Jew." This is an important observation, for the leadership models that are most attractive are charismatic: Gideon and Deborah, Elijah and Elisha; Amos and Hosea. But when it comes to telling the story of the diaspora community of faith surviving in a strange land the leadership model is plain and unassuming: a servant. When it is a matter of the survival, growth, and nurture of a community of God's people—which is the leadership task assigned to pastors—the servant is the model. Charismatic figures are raised up—given—to do special and important ministries. They must not be denigrated or devalued: they are sent by God to do his work. But they are inappropriate examples for *pastoral* practice. Pastors need to choose deliberately the servant style if they are to mature in ministry.

Pastors need to repudiate as models (though not as colleagues) persons who are promotional and glamorous. Jesus had a long and difficult struggle with his disciples over this issue. The story of the brothers Zebedee in Mark 10 is an instance. Reading between the lines we can reconstruct the brothers saying something like this: "We are among those few, privileged persons to whom God has made known his new way of life. He has commanded us to share this life with the world. We have been given authority over unclean spirits. The world desperately needs what we have to give. Obviously one of us has to be in charge. We will organize the people around us so that we can do the most effective job of sharing the good news."

There was no question about the importance of the work, their commitment to the challenge, their sense of having a ministry to exercise, their authority to do what had been commanded. They were confident; they were convinced; they were committed. There was a question, though, about how their authority would be exercised and in what tone of voice they would speak.

Jesus interrupted their argument with the words:

> "You know that those who are supposed to rule over the Gentiles lord it over them. . . . But it shall not be so among you; but whoever would be great among you must be your servant, and whoever would be first among you must be slave of all, for the Son of man also came not to be served but to serve, and to give his life as a ransom for many." (Mark 10:42–45)

Pastors need continuous retraining in servant work. For when a person is ordained to a position of authority there is a temptation to assert this authority in an imperialistic way, issuing commands instead of invitations, developing a superiority stance. "But it must not be so among you." Jesus was self-described as a servant. Paul's most frequent self-designation was "Paul, a servant . . . " Neither of them, though, originated the title. The Isaianic "servant songs" (Isa. 42:-1–9; 49:1–9; 50:4–11; 52:13—53:12) are the raw material out of which they constructed their servant roles. It is both possible and likely that they are also the source from which Mordecai learned to be a servant-leader. A careful exploration of these passages by pastors continues to be an important means for acquiring the habits and attitudes which distinguish pastoral work.

Brief comments on the first song will show some of the pastoral dimensions inherent in it.

> Behold my servant, whom I uphold,
>   my chosen, in whom my soul delights;
> I have put my Spirit upon him,
>   he will bring forth justice to the nations.
> He will not cry or lift up his voice,
>   or make it heard in the street;
> a bruised reed he will not break,
>   and a dimly burning wick he will not quench;
> he will faithfully bring forth justice.
> He will not fail or be discouraged
>   till he has established justice in the earth;
>   and the coastlands wait for his law.
>
> . . . .
> "I have given you as a covenant to the people,
>   a light to the nations,
>   to open the eyes that are blind,
> to bring out the prisoners from the dungeon,
>   from the prison those who sit in darkness." (Isa. 42:1–7)

This is particularly instructive because it combines a description of leadership style ("my servant . . .") with a charge to pastoral work ("'. . . open the eyes that are blind, to bring out the prisoners . . .' "). The style of pastoral leadership is as important as the content.

"Servant" is not a particularly difficult concept to grasp. It is, though, a difficult role to embrace. The word has low connotations. It is marked by loss of freedom, economic restrictions, and a demeaned status. No one *wants* to be a servant. A servant is the one who does things for others, usually things they don't want to do for themselves. "Servant" carries in its semantic train the unlovely underside of human existence. "Gospel" on the other hand is a word glowing with promise. It announces the power and majesty of God put to work for our redemption. It promises the best of eternity, with blessings spilling out on every facet of human existence. The kerygma is that God is doing something decisive in human existence. He is never inactive or silent. When the newspapers, though, fail to report what he is doing, those with a sense of responsibility for God's work are apt to generate a little news on their own—to make things happen that will catch the world's attention.

How dismaying then to find that the persons given responsibility for setting the "gospel" before a community of faith in preaching and teaching, must do it in the decidedly unspectacular role of servant: "though he was in the form of God, did not count equality with God a thing to be grasped, but emptied himself, taking the form of a servant. . . ." (Phil. 2:6–7) The God who in his majesty and strength is beyond our imaginations, who is glorious beyond belief, has chosen to work primarily in the form of a servant who is almost beneath our imaginations. "Behold my servant . . ." Servanthood, beyond cavil, is the leadership role.

Servants go about their work quietly and deferentially. They walk down the street and speak in soft, conversational tones.

> He will not cry or lift up his voice,
> or make it heard in the street. (Isa. 42:2)

There is no hard-sell and no loud argument with anyone who chooses to deny or ignore them. They go about their work in great gentleness. They will not destroy a "bruised reed," a person who counts for little in society's ledger. They will not coerce a person who might seem like a pushover ("a dimly burning wick"). There is no person, no matter how weak or useless, to whom they do not stand as servants. They at no time stand over another and bully. They stand under, or alongside. But they do it, also, as persons immersed in justice and law (mishpat and torah). They do it, in other words, as "a Jew."

Timothy L. Smith, the Johns Hopkins professor of history whose book, *Revivalism and Social Reform* is a benchmark study in American religious history, has commented on pastoral leadership thus:

It seems to me that we have applied production models to our view of church growth and church administration. Denominational leaders tend to think that the forward-looking pastor is the one who has a plan very much like a businessman's plan for saturating a market. Accordingly, we have stressed image and public relations too much, but I think that the great need is to recover a sense of the complexity and profundity of biblical truth.[37]

Some of that biblical truth has to do with the way God has always worked in his creation—as a servant. The nation Israel existed as a servant to the nations. Abraham was told "in you all the nations of the earth will be blessed." Battered by the political and military forces of the times, Israel nevertheless quietly, but effectively went about her servant task of providing a theology and a morality that are the foundations of human existence. We receive our politics, our science, our philosophy, and our economics from other nations and peoples, but Israel's faith serves us at our roots. She didn't do it by conquering but by being conquered. She didn't do it by shouting but by serving.

The servant role was completed in Jesus. Though there were auspicious signs that preceded and accompanied his birth, preparing the world for the majestic and kingly, the birth of Jesus itself was of the humblest peasant parentage, in an unimportant town, and in the roughest of buildings. He made a career of rejecting marks of status or privilege: he touched lepers, washed the feet of his disciples, befriended little children, encouraged women to join his entourage, and, finally, submitted to crucifixion by a foreign power. Everything about Jesus spoke of servitude: if Jesus is our model for leadership there can be no avoidance of the style by pastors.

Mordecai, of course, had no idea how God would use his servitude and his Jewishness. He was only confident that it would be used, even if not in the ways expected, and even if it would not appear effective to the Persian world—" 'for,' " he charged Esther, " 'if you keep silence at such a time as this, relief and deliverance will rise for the Jews from another quarter.' " (4:14) "Another quarter" *(maqom)* is most probably used here in its later sense as a substitute for the divine name.[38] God, never mentioned in the book of Esther, is everywhere assumed. A good servant doesn't call attention to him or herself.

Hadassah

It is probable that Hadassah, the Hebrew name for Esther (2:7) is not a proper name at all but a title, meaning "bride" (from the Akkadian *hadaššatu,* "bride").[39] If so, it is consistent with the extensive use of a biblical metaphor which designates God's people as his bride and emphasizes, in the telling of the Esther story, God's affection for and designs upon the community of faith, his people.

For the book of *Esther* is not important in the church because it tells the tale of the dubiously moral but stunningly beautiful Queen Esther, but in its dramatic, satisfying, and celebrative narration of the survival of God's people, God's *Hadassah,* in pagan Susa, despite Haman, through the ministry of Mordecai.

God works in community, which is to say that biblical religion is always and everywhere a community affair. It follows that pastoral work that is derivative from biblical sources is also a community affair. The promise to Abraham was that he would become a "people," " 'a great nation' " (Gen. 12:2), and " 'the father of a multitude of nations' " (17:4), and that " 'your descendants shall possess the gate of their enemies [*that* takes care of Haman!], and by your descendants shall all the nations of the earth bless themselves.' " (Gen. 22:17–18)

Salvation is experienced and faith articulated, always, from within the community (the *qahal*). There was common worship and common leadership. The question that had to be answered after the fall of Jerusalem and the Babylonian exile was: would these people be able to maintain their identity? Families were separated, traditions were destroyed, intermarriage had diluted racial purity. Would diaspora destroy community and turn biblical religion into cutthroat individualism? The answer is Esther. As far removed from Jerusalem as possible, out of touch with the flourishing exilic community in Babylon, intermarried in a pagan court (Esther, we must remember, was Xerxes' wife), the faith community was far from its root system, both physically and spiritually. As if that weren't enough, a deliberate program for annihilation was conceived by the arch enemy of the

Jews, Haman. Is it possible for God's community to survive when you remove it from its home base, when you take away its forms of worship, when you mix it into a pagan system, and subject it to powerful and malicious hostility?—even remove the name of God! The answer is "Yes, it is possible—let me tell you this story." Thomas Merton is serene in his witness: "The last thing in the world that should concern a Christian or the Church is *survival* in a temporal and worldly sense: to be concerned with this is an implicit denial of the Victory of Christ and of the Resurrection."[40]

Environment is important, culture is important, history is important. But none of these items is decisive. Always the faith community exists in an environment of unbelief. Environment, though, can neither account for the existence of God's people nor discount it. Which is to say that the sociologist cannot understand the church, the political scientist cannot understand the church, the journalist cannot understand the church. The reality of the church is not accessible to secular methods of analysis. Armchair historians survey the history of the life of God's people and generalize that certain periods were more or less favorable to the spiritual prosperity of the community. I can't see that anything in the culture makes much difference. What makes the difference is faithfulness, obedience, servanthood, prayer. It is no easier to be a Christian pastor in America than in Russia, China, or Zaire. Nor harder. It might be harder to be comfortable, to be learned, to be affluent, to be respected. But not harder to be a pastor.

While pastors need to be alert to the details of secularization in society, we must never be dismayed by them. Secularization does not threaten the existence of God's people. We can survive secularization as easily (and with as much difficulty) as we did Constantinianism. We can make it as an established church as well as a disestablished. We can survive in Susa as well as in Jerusalem as well as in Elephantine. Place and time are important because history is important and place and time provide the details and materials for actual obedience. But place and time are not decisive. As Dickens said of the French Revolution "It was the best of times, it was the worst of times . . ."[41] So, in some degree or another, is every time and place. Gerhard von Rad observed:

Israel threw off the vestment of her statehood together with her kingdom with surprising ease and without apparent internal crisis. This must be connected with the fact that the state as such was somewhat of a borrowed garment for Israel; for long before she became a state, she had belonged to Jahweh, and had at that time known herself as "the people of Jahweh." Thus, even after the destruction of her statehood, she could still think of herself as Jahweh's people.[42]

The nuptials between God and Hadassah take place in the unlikely setting of Susa. Cut off from the spiritual community in Babylon, separated from the historical traditions in Jerusalem, Esther, who is in the position to alter the course of affairs, has been assimilated into the harem, her Jewishness nearly obliterated by the intensive, twelve month beautification regiment of oil of myrrh, spices, and ointments (2:12). But it is not completely obliterated. Mordecai's daily inquiries at the gate, insignificant in appearance, are a high tensile thread of connection. The conclusion has all the ecstasy of a wedding: ". . . a day for gladness and feasting and holiday-making, and a day on which they send choice portions to one another." (9:19)

What else can this mean than that theology is indispensable for understanding God's community and that sociology is not; that God's people are constituted and preserved by grace not by culture. It makes little difference why persons think they come to church—whether to hear good music, to find a quiet place away from their kids, to get moral training for their children, to hear a good sermon, to be with the "better people" of the community. The actual reason that they assemble together is that God calls them. Pastors who know that are set free from competing with the fads of the people who stay away and from meeting the expectations of those who come. Pastors are set in a position of leadership among those whom God has called, in the assembly of those whom God preserves. This is not a moral community to be exhorted towards higher virtue; it is not an action community to be disciplined to heroic service; it is simply a fact—a people made and kept and continued by God. There is no evidence in Esther that the Jews even worship. The name of God is not mentioned in the book. The people do not have an objectively defined mission. They display no moral superiority, turning out as bad as the Persians in their readiness to kill. They are a *fact*, a creation, like all of God's creation, *ex nihilo*. Attempts to understand the church on any other grounds are doomed to failure. Max Weber can tell us many interesting things about the church but he can never account for it. The pastor must not fail to understand the congregation just as it is, as a historical community brought into being, warts and all, by God; and must not fail to be grateful for it, just as it is, warts and all, to God.

The most important single thing about the people of God is that they are *there*. They *exist*. They *are*, not because of favorable conditions in the empire, not because of certain perceived needs for which the church can provide a market, but because God called them out of nothing and made them a people (Hos. 1:10). They will continue for the same reason. Nothing can annihilate that creation, not Amelek, not Agag, not Haman, not Judas, not the Beast of the Apocalypse. Hadassah, the bride of Christ, is adorned for her husband:

"Hallelujah! For the Lord our God the Almighty reigns.
Let us rejoice and exult and give him the glory,
for the marriage of the Lamb has come,
and his Bride has made herself ready;
it was granted her to be clothed with fine linen, bright and pure."
                                                                (Rev. 19:6–8)

Praise, therefore, is the single most significant thing that the pastor can express in and for the community: not complaints, not moralism, not restlessness, not learning—but gratitude: Purim, a celebration of the survival and offering to God of the community of faith, the Hadassah.

EPILOGUE

A quest is not a conclusion. All pastoral work is work-in-progress. But neither is it aimless wandering. There is a goal. Along the way there are words that motivate, and light-filled moments that illuminate the next step. I have used the metaphor of stones now in two different ways to show how the biblical materials in general and the Megilloth in particular can be useful to pastors who are in quest of authenticity in their ministry: as foundation stones for constructing a substantial base upon which to build a parish ministry; and as gem stones which, when placed in the setting of kerygmatic worship, call attention to particular aspects of pastoral work in the body of Christ.

There is a third way to use the metaphor. A poem on 1 Samuel 17:31–40 by the Norwegian poet, Gunnar Thorkildsson, is full of suggestiveness for me as I listen for encouragement and look for direction in my pastoral work. The poem reads (my translation):

> Odd shaped pebbles roll
> and tumble 'round the Rock which
> smooths them into five smooth
> stones
> one of which will
> kill a giant.[1]

The image of the stones, waiting to be selected from the brook by David as he prepares for his meeting with Goliath, holds my attention. David has just discarded King Saul's armor as ill-fitting. The offer of bronze helmet and coat of mail was well-intentioned. But to accept it would have been disastrous. David needed what was authentic to him. Even as I do. For even though the weaponry urged upon me by my culture in the form of science and knowledge is formidable I cannot work effectively with what is imposed from the outside. Metallic forms hung on my frame will give me, perhaps, an imposing aspect but will not help me do my proper work.

And so I kneel at the brook of scripture, selecting there what God has long been preparing for the work at hand and find smooth stones. The rough edges have been knocked off. The soft parts have been eroded away. They are bare and hard. Nothing superfluous. Nothing decorative. Clean and spare. Scripture has that quality for me—of essentiality, of the necessary. I feel that I am, again, traveling light, delivered from an immense clutter.

David, in that moment at the brook, was at a point in history when the old leadership traditions were a shambles. The patriarchal, exodus, and wilderness traditions had all been developed in a nomadic culture. Now God's people were settled in a world that was agrarian and urban. The recent past in which charismatic judges had shown flashes of brilliance had disintegrated into anarchy. The attempt, out of that chaos, to establish order again through a monarchy was already on the way to failure. While David is at the brook Israel is at the point of losing its identity to the Philistines.

What strikes me so forcibly in that picture is that David was both modest enough and bold enough to reject the suggestion that he do his work inauthentically (by using Saul's armor); and that he was both modest enough and bold enough to use only that which he had been trained to use in his years as a shepherd (his sling and some stones). And he killed the giant.

It is a turning point in the story of God's ways with his people although no one knew it at the time. A new leadership ministry was taking shape. David was not yet king—it would be years before he was recognized as such. He was a marginal figure, even as the pastor is in our society, and slipped back into the obscurity of shepherding in the hill country. The world at that moment seemed divided between the arrogant and bully people of Philistia and the demoralized and anxious people of God, between the powerful but rather stupid giant and the anointed but deeply flawed king. No one could have guessed that the man picking stones out of the brook was doing the most significant work of the day.

NOTES

Introduction

1. Peter Marin, "The New Narcissism," *Harper's Magazine* 251, no. 1505 (October 1975):47.
2. "Any historical review of pastoral care . . . at once will heighten appreciation for the vast treasures that lie in the tradition, and will sharpen one's sense both of the uniqueness of human troubles that now arise and of the ever-novel ways in which soul care can be exercised. Much that past pastors have done was indeed ingenious, contemporaneous, rich, and creative, and becomes fresh and exciting in recollection." William A. Clebsch and Charles R. Jaekle, *Pastoral Care in Historical Perspective: An Essay with Exhibits* (New York: Jason Aronson, 1975), p. 2.
3. Donald G. Miller, *Fire in Thy Mouth* (Grand Rapids: Baker Book House, 1954), p. 83.
4. Saul Bellow, *Humboldt's Gift* (New York: Avon Books, 1976), p. 5.
5. Amos Niven Wilder, *Theopoetic: Theology and the Religious Imagination* (Philadelphia: Fortress Press, 1976), p. 83.
6. Herakleitos, "The Extant Fragments," tran. Guy Davenport, *The American Poetry Review*, January–February 1978, p. 14.
7. Clebsch and Jaekle, p. 76.
8. William Golding described his novel *Pincher Martin* as "a blow on behalf of the ordinary universe . . ." Quoted in Denis Donoghue, *The Ordinary Universe: Soundings in Modern Literature* (New York: The Macmillan Company, 1968), p. 9.
9. Lloyd R. Bailey, "The Lectionary in Critical Perspective," *Interpretation* 31, no. 2 (April 1977): 149.
10. C. S. Lewis, *The Allegory of Love* (New York: Oxford University Press, 1936), p. 1.
11. Gerhard von Rad, *Old Testament Theology: The Theology of Israel's Prophetic Traditions,* tran. D. M. G. Stalker (New York: Harper & Row, 1965), vol. 2, p. 328.
12. Ingmar Bergman in an interview said, " 'It is my opinion that art lost its basic creative drive the moment it was separated from worship. It

severed an umbilical cord and now lives its own sterile life, generating and degenerating itself. In former days the artist remained unknown and his work was to the glory of God . . . Today the individual has become the highest form and the greatest bane of artistic creation . . . The individualists stare into each other's eyes and yet deny the existence of each other . . .' " Quoted by Donald J. Drew, *Images of Man: A Critique of the Contemporary Cinema* (Downers Grove, IL: Inter-Varsity Press, 1974), p. 76. This observation is also true of pastoral work that is separated from worship.

13. Quoted by Bernard Bergonzi, *T. S. Eliot* (New York: Macmillan Co., 1972), p. 162.

14. Karl Barth, *Church Dogmatics* (Edinburgh: T & T Clark, 1962), vol. 4, part 3, second half, p. 501. Used with permission.

I. The Pastoral Work of Prayer-Directing: Song of Songs

1. Charles Williams, *The Descent of the Dove: A Short History of the Holy Spirit in the Church* (New York: Meridian Books, 1956), p. 131.

2. "*Redbook* magazine . . . reports on a computer analysis of 18,349 responses to a professionally prepared questionnaire on sexual attitudes and practices published in the magazine last fall . . . the survey does show that 'strongly religious' women report more sexual satisfaction, more orgasms and better communication with their husbands than 'fairly religious women.' At the bottom of the happiness scale are non-religious women; they are the least satisfied with the frequency and quality of intercourse, and the least likely to take an active role in lovemaking. *Redbook* editors admit to being 'astounded' by the correlation between religion and successful lovemaking. The magazine's theory is that more 'enlightened' clergymen have been teaching that sexual pleasure is 'a necessary element in a good marriage.' " (Reprinted by permission from TIME, The Weekly Newsmagazine; Copyright Time Inc. 1975; *Time* 106, no. 9 [September 1, 1975]: p. 62.) The editors' astonishment is puerile, and their explanation feeble. The correlation "between religion and successful lovemaking" is neither recent nor noteworthy—it is what pastors have known for centuries and for which they can take little credit. The "teaching" that sexual pleasure is a necessary element in a good marriage is not the discovery of the twentieth century, nor counselling it a speciality of "enlightened clergymen." The teaching is embedded in the biblical revelation (notably in The Song of Songs) and has been appreciated and acted upon by Christians and Jews for millenia.

3. Gerhard Kittel and Gerhard Friedrich, eds., *Theological Dictionary of the New Testament,* tran. Geoffrey W. Bromiley (Grand Rapids: Eerdmans Publishing House, 1971), vol. 7, p. 965. The emphasis is confirmed by Aulen: "Salvation . . . may be taken as a comprehensive term to describe man's new relation to God. . . . The classic idea of salvation is that the

victory which Christ gained once for all is continued in the work of the Holy Spirit, and its fruits reaped. So it is in the Fathers, and so it is in Luther; but it is typical of him that the finished work and the continuing work are even more closely connected together than before. The victory of Christ over the powers of evil is an eternal victory, therefore present as well as past. Therefore Justification and Atonement are really one and the same thing; Justification is simply the Atonement brought into the present, so that here and now the Blessing of God prevails over the Curse. It is therefore beside the point to argue whether *Christus pro nobis* or *Christus in nobis* is more emphasized, *propter Christum* or *per Christum;* for these are not two different things, but two sides of the same thing. Both are equally essential." Gustaf Aulén, *Christus Victor* (London: SPCK, 1950), p. 167.

4. "The *seder* ends with the recital of various psalms, the tasting of a fourth and final cup of wine, the singing of various hymns, and finally with popular songs dating from medieval times. In many communities the head of the household concludes the whole service by reading Canticles." Louis Finkelstein, *The Jews: Their History, Culture, and Religion* (New York: Harper & Brothers, 1955), vol. 2, p. 1367.

5. Lloyd R. Bailey, "The Lectionary in Critical Perspective," *Interpretation* 31, no. 2 (April 1977): 140.

6. Theodor H. Gaster, *Thespis: Ritual, Myth, and Drama in the Ancient Near East* (Garden City, NY: Doubleday/Anchor Books, 1961), p. 95.

7. James Bennett Pritchard, ed., *Ancient Near Eastern Texts: Relating to the Old Testament* (Princeton: Princeton University Press, 1955), p. 331ff.

8. Karl Barth, *Church Dogmatics,* vol. 3, part 1, p. 313.

9. Translation by Walther Eichrodt, *Ezekiel: A Commentary,* The Old Testament Library, tran. Cosslett Quinn (London: SCM Press Ltd., 1970), p. 199. (Italics removed by author.)

10. Barth, vol. 3, part 1, p. 313.

11. Wesley J. Fuerst, *The Cambridge Bible Commentary: The Books of Ruth, Esther, Ecclesiastes, The Song of Songs, Lamentations: The Five Scrolls* (Cambridge: Cambridge University Press, 1975), p. 168.

12. Theophile J. Meek, "Introduction and Exegesis of The Song of Songs," *The Interpreter's Bible,* ed. George Arthur Buttrick (Nashville: Abingdon Press, 1956), vol. 5, p. 92.

13. *Theological Dictionary of the New Testament,* vol. 1, p. 42.

14. Quoted in *Interpreter's Dictionary of the Bible,* vol. 4, p. 421.

15. *Ibid.,* p. 422.

16. C. S. Lewis, *The Voyage of the Dawn Treader* (New York: Macmillan Co., 1967), p. 177.

17. C. S. Lewis, *The Allegory of Love* (New York: Oxford University Press, 1936), p. 154.

18. Philip Rieff, *The Triumph of the Therapeutic: Uses of Faith After Freud* (New York: Harper & Row, 1966), p. 194.

19. ". . . sex and religion are intricately interwoven—for the Holy Grail, or cup, and the King's lance, of the Grail legends, were transparently sexual symbols—and myth was a kind of knowing . . ." Hyatt H. Wagoner, *American Poets* (New York: Houghton, 1968), p. 422.
20. Richard Wilbur, "Poplar, Sycamore" in *The Poems of Richard Wilbur* (New York: Harcourt Brace Jovanovich, Inc., 1963), p. 216. Used with permission.
21. Erich Auerbach, *Mimesis: The Representation of Reality in Western Literature,* tran. Willard R. Trask (Princeton: Princeton University Press, 1953), p. 555. Auerbach names this literary feature "figural interpretation" and describes it thus: "Figural interpretation 'establishes a connection between two events or persons in such a way that the first signifies not only itself but also the second, while the second involves or fulfills the first. The two poles of a figure are separated in time, but both, being real events or persons, are within temporality. They are both contained in the flowing stream which is historical life, and only the comprehension, the *intellectus spiritualis,* of their interdependence is a spiritual act.' " (P. 73)
22. Herman Melville, *Moby Dick* (New York: Bantam Books, 1967), p. 291.
23. Gerard S. Sloyan, "The Lectionary as a Context for Interpretation," *Interpretation* 31, no. 2 (April 1977): 133.
24. Meek, *The Interpreter's Bible,* vol. 5, p. 92.
25. Delbert R. Hillers, *Covenant: The History of a Biblical Idea* (Baltimore: John Hopkins Press, 1969), p. 5.
26. "In contrast to our civilization, the Hebrews lived in a world of the covenant rather than in a world of contracts. The idea of contract was unknown to them. The God of Israel 'cares as little for contract and the cash nexus as He cares for mere slavish obedience and obsequiousness. His chosen sphere is that of covenant.' His relationship to His partner is one of benevolence and affection. . . . God's life interacts with the life of the people. To live in the covenant is to partake of the fellowship of God and His people. Biblical religion is not what man does with his solitariness, but rather what man does with God's concern for all men." Abraham J. Heschel, *The Prophets* (New York: Harper & Row, 1962), p. 230.
27. Barth, vol. 3, part 1, p. 290.
28. Eugen Rosenstock-Huessy, *I Am an Impure Thinker* (Norwich, VT: Argo Books, Inc., 1970), p. 42.
29. Quoted in William Barclay, *A Spiritual Autobiography* (Grand Rapids: Eerdmans and Co., 1975), p. 100.
30. Quoted by Coventry Patmore, *The Rod, the Root and the Flower* (Freeport, NY: Books for Libraries Press, Inc., 1968), p. 123.
31. "The Prelude," book viii, ls. 279–281.

32. Barth, vol. 3, part 1, p. 290.
33. Robert Penn Warren, "Revelation," *Selected Poems 1923–1975* (New York: Random House, 1975). Used by permission. Copyright 1936, 1940, 1941, 1942, 1943, 1944, © 1955, 1957, 1958, 1959, 1960, 1963, 1965, 1966, 1967, 1968, 1969, 1970, 1971, 1972, 1973, 1974, 1975, 1976 by Robert Penn Warren. Copyright renewed, 1964, 1968, 1969, 1970, 1971, 1972 by Robert Penn Warren.
34. See Alfred Kazin, *On Native Grounds* (Garden City, NY: Doubleday & Co., Inc.), p. 170. Copyright, 1942, by Alfred Kazin.
35. Edward Dahlberg, *Can These Bones Live* (Ann Arbor: University of Michigan Press, 1967), p. xi.
36. Henri J. M. Nouwen, *Reaching Out: The Three Movements of the Spiritual Life* (Garden City, NY: Doubleday & Company, Inc., 1975), p. 30.
37. J. A. Jungmann, *Pastoral Liturgy* (London: Challoner Publications, Ltd., 1962), p. 386.
38. C. S. Lewis, *The Allegory of Love*, p. 157.
39. Anders Nygren, *Agape and Eros: A Study of the Christian Idea of Love* (London: SPCK, 1932), part 1, p. 54.
40. Dietrich Bonhoeffer, *Life Together* (New York: Harper & Row, 1954), p. 29.
41. Patmore, p. 68.

II. The Pastoral Work of Story-Making: Ruth

1. C. S. Lewis, penciled in the flyleaf of his copy of von Hugel's *Eternal Life;* quoted in Corbin Scott Carnell, *Bright Shadow of Reality: C. S. Lewis and the Feeling Intellect* (Grand Rapids: Eerdmans, 1974), p. 163.
2. Robert G. Boling, *Judges,* The Anchor Bible (Garden City, NY: Doubleday & Co., Inc., 1975), comment on chapter 19, pp. 277–279.
3. G. Ernest Wright, *The Old Testament Against Its Environment* (Chicago: Alec R. Allenson, Inc., 1950), pp. 68–69.
4. See William Foxwell Albright, *From the Stone Age to Christianity: Monotheism and the Historical Process* (Garden City, NY: Doubleday/Anchor, 1957) and John Bright, *A History of Israel* (Philadelphia: Westminster Press, 1959).
5. Edward F. Campbell, Jr., *Ruth,* The Anchor Bible (Garden City, NY: Doubleday & Co., 1975), pp. 8–9.
6. *Ibid.,* p. 80.
7. This is Erich Auerbach's phrase for the reality material that biblical writers uniquely introduced into Western literature. See his *Mimesis* (Princeton: Princeton University Press, 1953), p. 168.
8. Joseph Sittler, *The Ecology of Faith* (Philadelphia: Muhlenberg Press, 1961), p. 39.

9. G. Ernest Wright, *God Who Acts: Biblical Theology as Recital* (Chicago: Alec R. Allenson, Inc., 1960), p. 84.
10. Gilbert K. Chesterton, *Orthodoxy* (New York: John Lane Co., 1908), p. 254.
11. Gerhard von Rad, *Old Testament Theology* (New York: Harper & Row, 1965), vol. 2, p. 378.
12. Martin Thornton, *Pastoral Theology: A Reorientation* (London: SPCK, 1964), p. 270. Jonathan Edwards, a faithful pastoral visitor, refused to make what he called "tea and cake" calls, that is, calls that were socially expected.
13. Sheldon B. Kopp, *Guru: Metaphors from a Psychotherapist* (Palo Alto, CA: Science and Behavior Books, 1971), pp. 165–166.
14. Anonymous author, from *The Pilgrim Hymnal,* published in 1904.
15. Charles Williams, *The Descent of the Dove* (New York: Meridian Books, 1956), p. 205.
16. Campbell, p. 62.
17. Campbell, p. 83.
18. *Ibid.,* p. 116.
19. *Ibid.,* p. 114.
20. *Ibid.,* pp. 114–115.
21. *Ibid.,* p. 123.
22. *Ibid.,* p. 85.
23. *Ibid.,* p. 90.
24. *Ibid.,* p. 140.
25. *Ibid.,* p. 88.
26. *Ibid.,* p. 136.
27. Elie Wiesel, *Souls on Fire: Portraits and Legends of Hasidic Masters,* tran. Marion Wiesel (New York: Vintage Books, 1973), p. 99.
28. *Ibid.,* p. 170.
29. *Ibid.*
30. Thomas H. Johnson, ed., *The Complete Poems of Emily Dickinson* (Boston: Little, Brown, and Co., 1960), p. 153.
31. Cited by Peter Kreeft, "Zen Buddhism and Christianity: An Experiment in Comparative Religion," *Journal of Ecumenical Studies* 8 (1971): 532.
32. See W. F. Albright and C. S. Mann, *Matthew,* Anchor Bible (Garden City, NY: Doubleday & Co., Inc., 1971), p. 2, notes.
33. Roland Barthes, *The Pleasure of the Text,* tran. Richard Miller, (New York: Hill and Wang, a division of Farrar, Straus, and Giroux, 1975), p. 47.
34. C. S. Lewis, *Christian Reflections* (Grand Rapids: Eerdmans Publishing Co., 1967), p. 106.
35. Paul Goodman, *Little Prayers & Finite Experience* (New York: Harper & Row, 1972), p. 112.

36. Elie Wiesel, *The Gates of the Forest*, tran. Frances Frenaye (New York: Avon Books, 1974), p. 206.

III. The Pastoral Work of Pain-Sharing: Lamentations

1. Nicolas Berdyaev, *The Destiny of Man* (New York: Harper & Row, 1960), p. 193.
2. Philip Rieff, *The Triumph of the Therapeutic* (New York: Harper & Row, 1966).
3. Norman K. Gottwald, *Studies in the Book of Lamentations* (London: SCM Press, 1954), p. 23ff.
4. Norman Gottwald in *Interpreter's Dictionary of the Bible*, ed. George Arthur Buttrick (Nashville: Abingdon, 1962), vol. 3, p. 61.
5. Quoted by Delbert R. Hillers from H. Ewald, *Lamentations*, The Anchor Bible (Garden City, NY: Doubleday & Co., 1972), p. 64.
6. *Ibid.*, p. 86.
7. Quoted by Viktor E. Frankl, *Man's Search for Meaning* (New York: Simon and Schuster, 1962), p. 74.
8. Karl Barth, *The Epistle to the Romans* (London: Oxford University Press, 1960), p. 414.
9. Thornton Wilder, *Theophilus North* (New York: Harper & Row, 1973), p. 343.
10. W. H. Auden, "The Art of Healing" in E. Mendelson, ed., *Collected Poems* (New York: Random House, 1976), p. 626.
11. Peter R. Ackroyd, *Exile and Restoration: A Study of Hebrew Thought of the Sixth Century B.C.* (Philadelphia: Westminster Press, 1975), p. 45.
12. Gottwald, *Interpreter's Dictionary of the Bible*, vol. 3, p. 62.
13. Gerhard von Rad, *Old Testament Theology* (New York: Harper & Row, 1965), vol. 1, p. 109.
14. Wesley J. Fuerst, *The Cambridge Bible Commentary: The Books of Ruth, Esther, Ecclesiastes, The Song of Songs, Lamentations: The Five Scrolls* (Cambridge: Cambridge University Press, 1975), p. 45.
15. Abraham J. Heschel, *The Prophets* (New York: Harper & Row, 1962), p. 283.
16. *Ibid.*, p. 224.
17. C. S. Lewis, *Letters to Malcolm: Chiefly on Prayer* (New York: Harcourt Brace & World, 1964), p. 96.
18. Barth, *Romans*, pp. 419–420.
19. Harry Escott, ed., *The Cure of Souls: An Anthology of P. T. Forsyth's Practical Writings* (Grand Rapids: Eerdmans Publishing Co., 1971), p. 113.
20. Heschel, p. 193.
21. *Theological Dictionary of the New Testament*, vol. 5, p. 396

22. Walther Eichrodt, *Theology of the Old Testament,* tran. J. A. Baker (Philadelphia: Westminster Press, 1961), vol. 1, p. 265.
23. I heard the phrase from Karl Olssen, but don't know if it is in print.
24. Heschel, p. 179.
25. John Updike, *Rabbit, Run* (New York: Alfred A. Knopf, 1970), p. 237.
26. The Greek story of Philoctetes, the man with the stinking, incurable wound, whose invincible bow was indispensible for the taking of Troy, provides a mythic underpinning for the concept of the "wounded healer"—the person whose power to help is inseparable from participation in suffering. See Edmund Wilson, *The Wound and the Bow* (New York: Oxford University Press, 1965), pp. 223–242, and Henri J. M. Nouwen, *The Wounded Healer: Ministry in Contemporary Society* (New York: Doubleday & Co., 1972).
27. See Ivan Illich, *Medical Nemesis: The Expropriation of Health* (New York: Pantheon Books, a division of Random House, 1976), pp. 133–153.
28. Rieff, pp. 225–226.
29. Quoted by John T. McNeill, *A History of the Cure of Souls* (New York: Harper & Brothers, 1951), p. 244.
30. Frankl, p. 102.
31. Quoted by Frankl, p. 114.
32. C. S. Lewis, *The Problem of Pain* (New York: The Macmillan Publishing Co., 1953), p. 29.
33. Hillers, p. xxvii.
34. Homer, *The Iliad,* tran. Robert Fitzgerald (Garden City, NY: Anchor Press/Doubleday, 1974), p. 535.
35. Gottwald, *Interpreter's Dictionary of the Bible,* vol. 3, p. 62.
36. Günter Grass, *The Tin Drum,* tran. Ralph Manheim (New York: Pantheon, a division of Random House, Inc., 1961), p. 525.
37. Kornelis H. Miskotte, *When the Gods Are Silent,* tran. John W. Doberstein (London: Collins, 1967), p. 248.
38. Elie Wiesel, *The Gates of the Forest* (New York: Avon Books, 1974), p. 180.
39. Quoted by Colman McCarthy, *Inner Companions* (Washington, DC: Acropolis Books Ltd., 1975), p. 227.
40. Erik Routley, *Ascent to the Cross* (London: SCM Press Ltd, 1962), p. 29.
41. Denise Levertov, "Strange Song" in *The Freeing of the Dust* (New York: New Directions, 1975), p. 67.
42. Hillers, p. 50.
43. Quoted by Barth, *Romans,* p. 416.

IV. The Pastoral Work of Nay-Saying: Ecclesiastes

 1. Karl Barth, *The Epistle to the Romans* (London: Oxford University Press, 1960), p. 33.

2. R. B. Y. Scott, *Proverbs/Ecclesiastes,* The Anchor Bible (Garden City, NY: Doubleday & Co. Inc., 1965), p. 202.
3. Frank Zimmerman, *The Inner World of Qoheleth* (New York: KTAV Publishing House, 1973), p. 131.
4. Barth, *Romans,* p. 37.
5. John Bright, *A History of Israel* (Philadelphia: The Westminster Press, 1959), p. 427.
6. Sir Edwyn Hoskyns and Noel Davey, *The Riddle of the New Testament* (New York: Harcourt, Brace and Co., 1931), pp. 231–232.
7. Walther Eichrodt, *Theology of the Old Testament,* tran. J. A. Baker (Philadelphia: Westminster, 1961), vol. 2, p. 494.
8. George Aaron Barton, *The Book of Ecclesiastes,* The International Critical Commentary (Edinburgh: T & T Clark, 1908), p. 67. Henry Cazelles defines Qoheleth as "the man of the *qahal* [i.e., the congregation] who has charge of directing the holy community." "La titulature du roi David" *Melanges bibliques rediges en l'honneur de Andre Robert* (Paris, 1957), p. 135ff.
9. Eichrodt, vol. 2, p. 268.
10. O. S. Rankin, "Introduction and Exegesis to the Book of Ecclesiastes," *The Interpreter's Bible,* ed. George Arthur Buttrick (Nashville: Abingdon Press, 1956), vol. 5, p.4.
11. Robert Gordis, *Koheleth—The Man and His World* (New York: Schocken Books, 1973), p. 50.
12. *Ibid.,* p. 92.
13. *Theological Dictionary of the New Testament,* vol. 1, p. 338.
14. Louis Finkelstein, *The Jews: Their History, Culture, and Religion* (New York: Harper & Brothers, 1955), vol. 2, pp. 1368–1369.
15. There is a similar joining of opposites in the New Testament narration of Palm Sunday worship followed by the cursing of the fig tree and the cleansing of the temple. The Palm Sunday story has some Tabernacles material in it (the waving of the palms and the singing of Hosannas) and is purged of its superficiality and misunderstandings by the two negative acts. The Palm Sunday celebration is succeeded by a good housecleaning just as Tabernacles worship is scoured by Ecclesiastes.
16. W. Hertzberg, *Der Prediger ubersetzt und erklart* (Leipzig, 1932), p. 37ff.
17. Roland E. Murphy, "The Interpretation of Old Testament Wisdom Literature," *Interpretation* 23, no. 3 (July 1969): 289–301.
18. Herman Melville, *Moby Dick* (New York: Bantam Books, 1967), p. 392.
19. "What Melville wanted was a man who could 'say No! in thunder,' who had experienced not merely the mystery of life, but also its black tragedy. He had had 'enough of this Plato who talks thro' his nose' " [i.e., Emerson]. F. O. Matthiessen, *American Rennaisance: Art and Expression in the Age of Emerson and Whitman* (New York: Oxford University Press,

     1972), p. 186.
20. Saul Bellow, *The Adventures of Augie March* (New York: The Viking Press, 1953), p. 12.
21. Walter Harrelson, *Interpreting the Old Testament* (New York: Holt, Rinehart and Winston, Inc., 1964), p. 443.
22. T. S. Eliot, "Choruses from 'The Rock,'" COLLECTED POEMS 1909–1962, (New York: Harcourt Brace Jovanovich, Inc., 1963). Used by permission.
23. Howard Nemerov, "Lines & Circularities," *Gnomes & Occasions,* (Chicago: University of Chicago Press, 1973), p. 12.
24. See Amos N. Wilder, "Introduction and Exegesis to the First, Second, and Third Epistles of John" in *The Interpreter's Bible,* ed. George Arthur Buttrick, (Nashville: Abingdon, 1957), vol. 12, pp. 272–273.
25. Quoted by Garry Wills, *Chesterton: Man and Mask* (New York: Sheed & Ward, 1961), p. 196.
26. Eichrodt, vol. 1, pp. 173ff., 207ff., 219ff.; vol. 2, p. 270.
27. Diogenes Allen, "Miracles Old and New," *Interpretation* 28 (July 1974): 300. Used with permission.
28. See Eugene H. Peterson, "Baalism and Yahwism Updated," *Theology Today* 29, no. 2 (July 1972): 138ff.
29. Eichrodt, vol. 1, p. 101.
30. See the discussion on the relation of liturgy to life in Dom Gregory Dix, *The Shape of the Liturgy* (London: Dacre Press, 1960), p. xviii.
31. Charles Williams, *The Descent of the Dove* (New York: Meridian Books, 1956), p. 5.
32. "If I were a printer, I should certainly undertake the issuance of an edition of the New Testament with the book of Ecclesiastes bound in with it, just preceding the Gospel of Matthew, as the book of Psalms is frequently sold with the New Testament." Floyd E. Mallot, *Is Life Worth Living?* (Elgin, IL: The Brethren Press, 1972), p. 8.
33. Gerhard von Rad, *Old Testament Theology,* tran. D. M. G. Stalker (New York: Harper & Row, 1965), vol. 1, p. 45C.
34. Quoted by E. W. Hengstenberg, *Commentary on Ecclesiastes* (Philadelphia: Smith, English, and Co., 1869), p. 31.
35. Raymond Bernard Blakney, *Meister Eckhart: A Modern Translation* (New York: Harper & Brothers, 1941), p. 53.

V. The Pastoral Work of Community-Building: Esther

  1. Martin Buber, *I and Thou,* tran. Walter Kaufmann (New York: Charles Scribner's Sons, 1970), p. 94.
  2. Karl Barth, *Church Dogmatics,* vol. 4, part 3, second half, p. 743.
  3. John A. T. Robinson, *The Body: A Study in Pauline Theology* (London: SCM Press, Ltd, 1952), p. 15.

4. Louis Finkelstein, *The Jews: Their History, Culture, and Religion* (New York: Harper & Brothers, 1955), vol. 2, p. 1373.
5. Bernhard W. Anderson, "Introduction and Exegesis of Esther," *The Interpreter's Bible* (Nashville, Abingdon, 1954), vol. 3, p. 829.
6. Ellen Glasgow, *The Sheltered Life* (Garden City, NY: Doubleday, Doran & Company, Inc., 1934), p. 46.
7. Henri J. M. Nouwen, *Creative Ministry* (New York: Doubleday and Co., Inc., 1971), p. 99.
8. D. H. Lawrence, *Studies in Classic American Literature* (Garden City, NY: Doubleday Anchor Books, Doubleday & Co., Inc., 1953), p. 17.
9. There is also a reference to a Jewish diaspora community at Sardis, capital of Lydia in Asia Minor—in Aramaic probably from the year 455, reflecting a settlement of a Jewish Aramaic community in that place. See William F. Albright, *The Biblical Period* (Pittsburgh: University of Pennsylvania, 1950), p. 63.
10. William Foxwell Albright, *Archaeology and the Religion of Israel* (Baltimore: The Johns Hopkins Press, 1956), p. 168.
11. William F. Albright, *Recent Discoveries in Bible Lands* (New York: Funk and Wagnalls Co., 1955), p. 101.
12. Gillis Gerleman, *Esther*, Biblischer Kommentar Altes Testament, XXI, 1–2 (Neukirchen-Fluyn: Neukirchener Verlag des Erziehungsvereins, 1970–73), p. 43.
13. John Bright, *A History of Israel* (Philadelphia: Westminster Press, 1959), p. 360.
14. G. Ernest Wright, *Biblical Archaeology* (Philadelphia: Westminster Press, 1957), p. 207.
15. Bengel, quoted by Alexandre Rudolphe Vinet, *Pastoral Theology: The Theory of the Evangelical Ministry*, tran. Thomas H. Skinner (Edinburgh: T & T Clark, 1852), p. 301.
16. Andrew A. Bonar, ed., *The Letters of the Rev. Samuel Rutherford* (Edinburgh: Oliphant, Anderson & Ferrier, 1891), p. 80.
17. Erik Routley, *Words, Music and the Church* (Nashville: Abingdon Press, 1968), p. 219.
18. Martin Thornton, *Pastoral Theology: A Reorientation* (London: SPCK, 1964), p. 164.
19. Quoted by Bernard M. G. Reardon, "The Doctrine of the Church in Recent Catholic Theology," *Expository Times* 88 (March 1977): 166.
20. Quoted by James S. Stewart, *The Strong Name* (London: Hodder and Stoughton, 1941), p. 145.
21. John Bright, *The Kingdom of God: The Biblical Concept and Its Meaning for the Church* (Nashville: Abingdon Press, 1953), p. 178.
22. Thornton, p. 138.
23. Martin Noth, *The History of Israel* (London: A & C Black, 1959), pp. 301–306

24. *Ibid.,* p. 305.
25. Wright, p. 206.
26. See Reinhold Niebuhr, "Why Is Barth Silent on Hungary?" *Christian Century* (January 23, 1957); and "Barth on Hungary: An Exchange," *Christian Century* (April 10, 1957).
27. G. Johannes Botterweck and Helmer Ringgren, eds., *Theological Dictionary of the Old Testament,* tran. John T. Willis, (Grand Rapids: Eerdmans Publishing Co., revised edition, 1977), vol. 1, p. 218.
28. *Theological Dictionary of the New Testament,* vol. 2, p. 813.
29. "Men of little faith"—a frequent designation by Jesus of his disciples when they failed to trust in the overwhelming providence of God (Matthew 6:30; 8:26; 14:31; 16:8).
30. For a theology of the "holy war" (herem) see Gerhard von Rad, *Der Heilige Krieg im alten Israel* (Zürich: Zwingli-Verlag, 1951). It is significant, I think, that the most complete and detailed accounts ("die weitaus reichste Quelle," p. 68) of the holy war are in the Deuteronomic material which is also richest in pastoral traditions. Those who were concerned with developing the identity and integrity of a worshiping community which was practiced in love were also most alert to what threatened that community, within and without, and were in possession of a theology of absolute reliance on God's intervention. For it must not be overlooked that the theology of the holy war was *never* a rationale for aggressive militarism, but always was a trust in the God who would take care of the enemy. All that was required of Israel was trust and obedience. "Jahweh himself went into battle and defeated the enemy by means of the divine terror he sent upon them." (von Rad) A holy war theology did not produce a militaristic people but a people who had lost all naivete about evil and were single-minded, undistracted, and ardent in matters of faith.
31. The phrase, along with perceptive instances of its meaning, is found in Sheldon Vanauken, *A Severe Mercy* (New York: Harper & Row, 1977).
32. Hans Wilhelm Hertzberg, *I & II Samuel: A Commentary,* The Old Testament Library, tran. J. S. Bowden (Philadelphia: Westminster Press, 1964), p. 128.
33. Esther 2:5; 3:4; 5:13; 6:10; 8:7; 9:29, 31; 10:3.
34. W. B. Yeats, "Municipal Gallery Revisited," *The Collected Poems of W. B. Yeats* (New York: Macmillan, 1959), p. 318.
35. Henri J. M. Nouwen, *Reaching Out* (New York: Doubleday & Co., 1975), p. 20.
36. Garry Wills, *Bare Ruined Choirs: Doubt, Prophecy and Ruined Religion* (Garden City, NY: Doubleday & Co., Inc., 1972), p. 249.
37. Timothy L. Smith, "A 'Fortress Mentality': Shackling the Spirit's Power," *Christianity Today* 21, no. 4 (November 19, 1976): 24.
38. See the discussion in Hans Bardtke, *Das Buch Esther* (Gütersloher:

Verlagshaus Gerd Mohn, 1963), pp. 332–333.
39. *Interpreter's Dictionary of the Bible,* vol. 2, p. 508. This is, admittedly, a
minority opinion. Most scholars accept the Targumic tradition which
interprets Hadassah as "myrtle" because, says Targum II, "as the myrtle
spreads fragrance in the world, so did she spread good works. And for
this cause she was called in the Hebrew language Hadassah because the
righteous are likened to myrtle." (Quoted in Moore, op. cit., p. 20.)
40. Thomas Merton, *Conjectures of a Guilty Bystander* (Garden City, NY:
Image Books, Doubleday & Co., Inc., 1968), p. 126.
41. Charles Dickens, *A Tale of Two Cities* (New York: New American
Library, Signet Classic, 1936), p. 13.
42. Gerhard von Rad, *Old Testament Theology,* tran. D. M. G. Stalker (New
York: Harper & Row, 1965), vol. 1, p. 90.

Epilogue

1. Gunnar Thorkildsson, "Discipleship," trans. Eugene Peterson, *Christianity Today* (September 10, 1971). Copyright ©1971 *Christianity
Today.*